D0949436

PRESENTED TO:

Patty

Love FROM:

Fred + Gloria

DATE:

Christmas 2003

WOMEN

LIVING A LIFE OF PURPOSE...

GOD'S WAY

WHITE STONE BOOKS
LAKELAND, FLORIDA

UNLESS OTHERWISE INDICATED, SCRIPTURE QUOTATIONS ARE TAKEN FROM THE *KING JAMES VERSION* OF THE BIBLE.

SCRIPTURE QUOTATIONS MARKED (NKJV) ARE TAKEN FROM *THE NEW KING JAMES VERSION*® NKJV®. COPYRIGHT© 1979, 1980, 1982, THOMAS NELSON, INC. ALL RIGHTS RESERVED.

SCRIPTURE QUOTATIONS MARKED (NIV) ARE TAKEN FROM THE HOLY BIBLE, *NEW INTERNATIONAL VERSION*®. NIV®. COPYRIGHT © 1973, 1978, 1984 BY THE INTERNATIONAL BIBLE SOCIETY. USED BY PERMISSION OF ZONDERVAN PUBLISHING HOUSE. ALL RIGHTS RESERVED.

SCRIPTURE QUOTATIONS MARKED (NLT) ARE TAKEN FROM THE HOLY BIBLE, *NEW LIVING TRANSLATION*, COPYRIGHT © 1996. USED BY PERMISSION OF TYNDALE HOUSE PUBLISHERS, INC., WHEATON, ILLINOIS 60189. ALL RIGHTS RESERVED.

VERSES MARKED (TLB) ARE TAKEN FROM *THE LIVING BIBLE* © 1971. USED BY PERMISSION OF TYNDALE HOUSE PUBLISHERS, INC., WHEATON, ILLINOIS 60189. ALL RIGHTS RESERVED.

SCRIPTURE QUOTATIONS MARKED (NASB) ARE TAKEN FROM THE *NEW AMERICAN STANDARD BIBLE*. COPYRIGHT © THE LOCKMAN FOUNDATION 1960, 1962, 1963, 1968, 1971, 1972, 1973, 1975, 1977, 1995. USED BY PERMISSION.

SCRIPTURE QUOTATIONS MARKED (RSV) ARE TAKEN FROM *THE REVISED STANDARD VERSION BIBLE*, COPYRIGHT © 1946, OLD TESTAMENT SECTION COPYRIGHT © 1952 BY THE DIVISION OF CHRISTIAN EDUCATION OF THE NATIONAL COUNCIL OF THE CHURCHES OF CHRIST IN THE UNITED STATES OF AMERICA. USED BY PERMISSION.

07 06 05 04 03   10 9 8 7 6 5 4 3 2

WOMEN - LIVING A LIFE OF PURPOSE...GOD'S WAY
ISBN 1-59379-006-6
COPYRIGHT © 2003 JOHN M. THURBER
THURBER CREATIVE SERVICES, INC.
TULSA, OKLAHOMA

EDITORIAL DEVELOPMENT AND LITERARY REPRESENTATION BY
MARK GILROY COMMUNICATIONS, INC.
6528 E. 101ST STREET, SUITE 416
TULSA, OKLAHOMA 74133-6754

EDITORIAL MANAGER: CHRISTY STERNER

PUBLISHED BY WHITE STONE BOOKS, INC.
P.O. BOX 2835
LAKELAND, FLORIDA 33806

PRINTED IN THE UNITED STATES OF AMERICA. ALL RIGHTS RESERVED UNDER INTERNATIONAL COPYRIGHT LAW. CONTENTS AND/OR COVER MAY NOT BE REPRODUCED IN WHOLE OR IN PART IN ANY FORM WITHOUT THE EXPRESS WRITTEN CONSENT OF THE PUBLISHER.

NTRODUCTION

He has made His wonderful works to be remembered.
PSALM 111:4 NKJV

God is faithfully at work today in the lives of people around the world—revealing His ways, demonstrating His power, and expressing His infinite love. Do you know that He wants to do the same for you?

Are you looking for answers to the many questions you deal with as a woman?

Do you need a generous helping of encouragement to assist you in handling the challenges of life? Perhaps you are facing pressures in a career, in raising children, or in building a family. Do you need a touch from God to succeed with grace and poise?

Maybe you simply need a reminder of how God is at work in the world changing lives today—including yours.

God's Way for Women is filled with true, personal stories that present spiritual insights from women experiencing the same range of life situations you face; from women who have looked to God for help and hope—and received it.

Prepare to encounter new levels of power and grace in your life as you experience what it means to live a life of purpose…*God's Way.*

ONTENTS

WOMEN
LIVING A LIFE OF PURPOSE...
GOD'S
WAY

ℰARLS OF TIME

KAREN MARJORIS-GARRISON

Similarly, teach the older women to live in a way that is appropriate for someone serving the Lord. They must not go around speaking evil of others and must not be heavy drinkers. Instead, they should teach others what is good. These older women must train the younger women to love their husbands and their children.

TITUS 2:3-4 NLT

"WHEN GRACE IS JOINED WITH WRINKLES, IT IS ADORABLE. THERE IS AN UNSPEAKABLE DAWN IN HAPPY OLD AGE."

Victor Hugo

I hadn't intended to isolate myself in my bedroom for three days, but the unexpected death of a dear friend devastated me. As a new Christian, I felt unprepared for the questions and doubts that overwhelmed me.

The door opened and my husband, Jeff, came in.

"It's going to be okay," he said softly, stroking my hair.

I buried my head in his shoulder. I didn't understand this grief. Life had seemed so perfect until this happened. One minute Jeff and I were rejoicing in the news of my pregnancy, the next, we grieved the loss of a friend. The future was an uncertain destiny. *How was I, a Christian woman and now expectant mother, supposed to view life's sorrows and triumphs?* I wondered.

"I'm so confused," I confessed, lifting my tear-streaked face. "I wish God would just give me a simple answer. A vision of how to journey through life as a Christian woman."

Just then, the doorbell rang. Jeff kissed the top of my head, and left to answer it. When slow-moving footsteps returned to the doorway, I was surprised to find my elderly neighbor, Sarah, appraising me. I yearned for the wisdom her blue eyes carried behind wire-rimmed glasses.

"I missed your visits the past few days," she said, shuffling over to sit beside me. "I thought you might be experiencing morning sickness, but then I learned of your friend's death."

I didn't say a word. Sarah was the godliest woman I had ever met, but she rarely left her home unless it was an emergency. I suppose she figured this was an emergency.

"How do I look today?" she surprised me by asking.

"Beautiful," I answered, assessing her pale blue dress and pearl necklace. "I've never seen that necklace before. It's lovely."

"You have one too," she said, briefly lifting a finger to point at my collarbone. "Only it's a spiritual one unseen by human eyes." She reached behind her neck and unlocked the necklace. Holding it between her fingers, she rubbed the pearls gently. "This necklace was given to me as a reminder of the heavenly necklaces women wear." Patting my knee, she met my gaze and continued, "God instilled in women an incredible sense of caring and compassion, Karen. We are the nurturers, the vessels of life. We take care of our husbands, our children, our homes, and sometimes we feel as though everyone's emotional well-being depends on us."

She paused, handing me a tissue, then smiled. "Long ago, when I was a child, an elderly woman told me that she believed there's a special blessing for women—a "pearls-of-time" necklace that we're born with. During our lifetime, the pearls that adorn our necks represent momentous events in our lives."

Moved by her words, I instinctively touched my neck, as if I could sense adornment there.

"But," she emphasized, holding the necklace for me to see, "the most important part is the clasp that holds it together. That represents Jesus. Like a perfect circle—from beginning to end—He's with us, holding us firmly throughout life's tragedies and triumphs. We only need to remember and trust in that." She sighed, slipping the necklace back on and waiting for me to speak.

Speechless, I absorbed her words, allowing them to soothe

my soul. "I don't know what to say," I whispered.

"Don't say anything, then," she chuckled, standing up. "I'm just obeying the Scripture that says that older women should be holy and teach the younger ones. One day you will, too. Right now, you're a young, Christian woman with a teachable spirit and a great desire to obey God. That's a winning combination."

We embraced, and I inhaled the familiar scent of lilac soap. "Thank you, Sarah. Thank you."

"You don't have to thank me, honey," she said, "but I do have to go. My son is waiting." She was almost out of the doorway, when she stopped briefly and turned to me. Lifting her hand, she brought my attention to her neck. "Just remember, dear."

"I will," I promised, walking over to help her down the stairs.

As I watched the car disappear around a curve, I suddenly felt renewed. "Thank You, Jesus," I whispered, closing my eyes. "Thank You for answering my prayers." When I reopened them, my vision was clear.

Four years later, I clutched the hand of my three-year-old daughter, Abigail, as we stood beside the hospital bed that Sarah was lying in. "You're going to get better," I told her, watching in despair, as her face grew more pale.

"I'm not worried, dear," she grinned, squeezing my hand.

"I'm looking forward to seeing the Lord."

"But we'll miss you," I blurted, clutching her hand. "I love you! You've not only been my friend, but you've been my teacher. I'll miss our talks, our laughter, our—"

"Shhh," she smiled, meeting my eyes. "You'll do just fine without me." She pointed to a small box lying on the bedside table. "Take that. Open it tonight with Abigail. It'll help both of you. Now, promise me."

"I promise," I said, slipping the box into my purse.

We said our tearful good-byes, as I tried to be more lighthearted for Abigail's sake, but Sarah and I both knew it would be the last time we'd see each other.

Later that night, after receiving the news that Sarah had passed away, I snuggled with Abigail on the couch. She curled into my side, her silky hair brushing against my cheek. "Open it, Mama," she said, curiously touching the box.

Through tear-filled eyes, I lifted the lid and found the pearl necklace that Sarah had modeled for me so many years ago.

"It's beautiful, Mommy," Abigail exclaimed, gently touching the shimmering treasure. "But why do I still feel so sad? Sarah said we'd feel better."

Her question tugged at my heart, but I was prepared. And with awe, I realized that Sarah had thought of everything. She had passed on to me a priceless gift, knowing that Abigail would have questions that I'd have to answer. "Well, honey," I said, touching her soft cheek with my fingertips, "I don't think the hurt will ever fully go away, but Jesus will see us through it. Sarah once told me a story about necklaces—'pearls-of-time' necklaces. Would you like to hear it?"

After her exuberant nod, I imagined my own invisible necklace, having a new, shimmering pearl this day from my sadness at Sarah's death. It would be placed right beside the pearls of joy from my wedding, Abigail's birth, and later, happily marking the day my son, Simeon, was born.

Abigail lifted her small fingers and touched my face. I peered down into her beautiful, dark eyes and began. "Well," I smiled, loving every inch of her, "when little girls are born...."

MIRACLE IN THE RAIN

JAN COLEMAN

And we know that God causes everything to work together for the good of those who love God and are called according to his purpose for them.

ROMANS 8:28 NLT

"THINGS WILL PROBABLY COME OUT ALL RIGHT, BUT SOMETIMES IT TAKES STRONG NERVES JUST TO WATCH."
Hedley Donovan

"My daughter drove furiously up a mountain freeway in a rainstorm. Her vehicle hydroplaned and flipped upside down, along with my world as I knew it.

Carl and I inched our way to the hospital, driving through gushing streams of water. I was numbed by the news of Jennifer's accident. Carl was silent. We knew no details, only that Jennifer had been airlifted to a trauma center twenty miles away.

My heart cried out, *Please, Lord, don't let my daughter die with a wall between us.*

For the past year, Jen had been on a mad dash from her problems. With her marriage unraveling, her natural spunk turned every family gathering into a sparring match.

Outwardly she seemed shockproof, in complete control, but inside Jennifer was still a fragile young girl with broken dreams, aching for the father who had abandoned his family years ago. I tried to mend the wounds in her life with a mother's counsel and correction, but my unwelcome words only made her more defensive.

She hadn't spoken to me in more than two months.

At the hospital, the neurosurgeon grimly said, "Surprisingly, she has only a few broken ribs, but she does have a serious head injury." She was in "bad shape." His dismayed look said it all. He didn't think she would make it.

So this is where the rubber meets the road when it comes to faith, Lord?

When we entered the hospital chapel, we found her husband, Steve. "We had a terrible fight last night, and I said some awful things." He spoke the words—his face filled with pain.

As I sobbed, Romans 8:28 came to mind: "All things work together for good...." How many times had I spouted that verse to someone in crisis? Did I really believe it now?

All things? Even tragic car accidents?

Then it hit me. Fretting would not change the outcome. Panicking would do no good. If I trusted God, as I claimed I did, I must cast all doubts aside. My daughter's life was in God's hands. My heart breaking, I told God, *I trust You, no matter what. I'll praise You, no matter what.* That was the toughest thing I ever promised to do.

Jen lay in a coma, her swollen, shaved head hooked to tubes, wires, and pressure monitors. Machines blipped and beeped while nurses worked frantically to keep her blood pressure stable. If not, death could steal her at any moment. And even if she did survive, brain damage was likely.

God, give me Your perspective on this. My spiritual eyes are too blurry. I looked up and saw Jenny, so peaceful, so beautiful. God seemed to be restoring her soul while she slept.

A voice pulled me from my thoughts. "How's my girl?" a young hospital technician asked.

"I was at the accident scene with this little lady," Phillip then told me.

He'd been heading down the mountain when he saw a massive crash ahead and a tiny dot catapult from the sunroof of a car; it was Jennifer, whose body crash-landed on the freeway just inches from her mangled vehicle.

"It took me three, four minutes to get there," Phillip explained. "I was late to work, but something told me I had to stop." He saw the highway patrol officer cover Jen's curled, lifeless body with a yellow slicker. Turning to call the coroner, the officer waved Phillip away. "She's not going to make it." But Phillip shot back, "I won't believe that!"

Trained as a Navy field medic, he went to work on my daughter. Finally, she gasped a breath. But it wouldn't be enough. Her only hope was in the rescue helicopter that hovered in the sky, unable to land because of the fierce rain and wind that battered the roadway. Just then another car pulled up, an off-duty EMT who had seen the commotion. He just happened to have a respirator in his car.

Minutes later, the storm quieted, and the helicopter landed.

I imagined an image of Jesus darting to catch Jennifer, His body cushioning her against a deadly fall that could have broken her body. I envisioned the Savior prompting Phillip to stop, directing the scene, clearing the raging skies for the circling helicopter.

Then I knew what it meant to have a peace that passes all understanding.

According to the doctor's charts, Jennifer's condition was not a hopeful one. It didn't matter. God works from His own heavenly charts.

Carl and I arrived for church early the next day to update our pastor on Jen's condition. God reached down and hugged us through the arms of the congregation. When I opened the bulletin I shook my head in disbelief: The title of the sermon was "God's Purpose for My Problems," the message being, that how we respond to problems reveals what we believe about God.

All we could do was pray and wait. But I had a silent hopefulness that had no earthly explanation, and all my friends asked me, "Are you in shock?"

God was at work, and I was in awe of what He would do next.

A few days later my former husband, whom we hadn't seen in seven years, showed up at the hospital. Taking one look at his Jennifer on a breathing machine, he hung his head. "Can we talk somewhere?"

I sat facing the man who'd ripped my heart out, who'd turned his back on his young children.

"If I hadn't walked out on you," he said, "none of this would have happened. She's just like me, reckless and immature, running away from herself. I'm sorry I messed up our marriage, Jan. You were a good wife. None of this would be happening if I hadn't left you. Will you forgive me?"

How I'd dreamt of hearing those very words, but now thinking, *his concern comes awfully late.* I wanted to launch into a full report, make sure he knew all the details of the struggles we'd had because of his selfish choices, how his daughters were forever scarred, but those words wouldn't come out. All I could manage to utter was, "I forgave you long ago," and we wept together.

As God's grace poured over me, the last remnants of my

own pain melted away

I couldn't sleep that night; my emotions shifted like a flag tossed in the wind. I'd wanted my daughters to be restored to their father, but now I was troubled by it. Jennifer was just beginning to bond with my husband, Carl. And now her biological dad, had come waltzing in, right in the middle of the crisis, sincere at the moment, but would he follow through and hurt her again?

As I laid anxious and awake, I felt the Lord tug at my heart, *Jan, I'm in control. Leave the results up to Me.*

The next day, Jen twitched a foot and began to emerge from the coma. The doctors shook their heads in amazement. Not only was she not paralyzed, she would recover. "A miracle," they said. Ten days later we transferred her to a rehabilitation hospital.

The doctors said they'd never seen such progress after a brain injury. Jen's fighting spirit played in her favor now, kicking in while she pushed to walk, formulate sentences, even chew her food again. The staff had never seen such amazing progress.

There was a refreshing softness to my daughter, one I hadn't seen since she was a child. One day as I sat by her bed and stroked her half-shaved curls, her words touched my heart: "Mom, I never want to fight with you again. I realize how much you love me and want the best for me. I want to learn how to be a better wife and grow closer to God."

Three months after the accident, Jennifer walked shakily into her own house, back to Steve and two young sons. And now, five years later, she's made almost a full recovery from a severe brain injury.

I look at my daughter differently now. While Jen's strength and determination were a past source of conflict for me, I now see they are actually gifts from God, and He intends to use them to do great things in her life. My daughter is a precious stone in the Master's hand that He is crafting for His glory. And He doesn't need my help. I've given up my advice-giving. I've stopped trying to fix her. I seek God's perspective first. That's the way to find the purpose in our problems.

People in our small town still talk about "the miracle in the rain," the rescue, the amazing recovery.

But to me there is still yet another miracle—having my daughter as my friend.

THE YEAR OF THE UNEXPECTED

MELINDA TOGNINI

And we know that all things work together for good, to them that love God.

ROMANS 8:28

"IT IS OFTEN HARD TO DISTINGUISH BETWEEN THE HARD KNOCKS OF LIFE AND THOSE OF OPPORTUNITY."

Frederick Phillips

"They've found a tumor. It's about as bad as it gets."

It was not the news I had expected to hear. My father, on his biannual trip to visit us from Papua, New Guinea, had spent the day in the hospital undergoing what were supposed to be routine tests. He'd assumed the doctor would find and remove a few ordinary polyps from his bowel. Now we were hearing the C word. Further tests were needed. Hope seemed dependent on whether or not the tumor had spread to his liver. If so, then there was little that could be done.

I was numb. I didn't know what to think. It wasn't the first time someone I knew had been faced with cancer.

I just didn't expect it to be my dad. He'd always been so

healthy and fit from a life of camping, hiking, and sailing.

Chemo and radiation therapy began. A two-week holiday turned into two months of fierce battle against cancer. We received good news—the tumor was contained in the bowel, but the fight continued.

Several weeks after Dad's initial diagnosis, I was quietly reflecting on our situation, when I had an unexpected thought, *God will provide.* What did this thought mean? Was it possible that God was actually speaking to me, or was it just a random idea that had gone through my mind?

A few days later, my husband called from work.

"I'm on my way home. I've just lost my job."

Things looked grim. When we looked over our financial situation, we saw that we had enough money to last three weeks if we only bought the basics, and if no emergency arose.

That first week my sister-in-law brought us groceries. Someone else gave us fresh bread. Then the school at which I'd previously worked offered both of us relief work. My husband, an experienced accountant, found several new clients. In addition, my deputy principal commissioned me to write a play, an opportunity that might not have occurred had it not been for our situation. It became a scenario of living week to week, but we earned enough to just get by.

I received the opportunity to become the assistant chaplain

at our school, two days a week. I wouldn't have considered the job had my husband been working full-time, but now he could look after our son while I worked. Later I discovered that two other staff members had desired the position because it meant that they could work part-time. If my husband had not lost his job when he did, the job opening might not have been there for me to provide for our family while my husband gradually built his own business.

My husband's business continues to grow, and it allows him to spend more time with his son than most fathers. I was able to go back to work at a school I love with students I think are fantastic and still have time at home with my family.

During all of these changes, my dad continued cancer treatment. I saw him as much as I possibly could. I calculated that if we usually only saw him for two weeks every two years, then all of the time we now spent together had given us a decade worth of visits together. This time spent between my son and my father firmly cemented the bond between both of them.

With Dad's health fund overseas, it complicated things. He had to pay his massive medical bills up front with money he did not have. My grandparents, who usually lived on a tight budget, had just sold their house, which afforded the much-needed finances to cover Dad's bills.

Major surgery came with a slice right down the middle of

his stomach. He spent days in "special care," a week on and off oxygen, and yet another week before he could be released. Waiting for the pathology results was nerve-wracking. Would they be promising or devastating? It was the toughest time of Dad's life.

The results were positive. The chemo and radiation therapy had shrunk and softened the tumor so that the surgeon was able to remove it all. But the fight wasn't over yet. There would be more chemotherapy to come, further surgery, and then a six-month wait for the checkup that we hoped would give him the all clear.

Those months were challenging to say the least. We wondered if we'd have enough money to last the next week. And even worse, I wondered if each day was the last time I would see Dad.

I believe without a doubt that I had heard from God that day I sat and quietly reflected with an unexpected thought of *God will provide*. He kept His promise. He provided. He provided money as we needed it. We realized how much we took for granted and how much we had previously wasted. He provided the finances my father needed, too. He supplied people to support my Dad as he battled cancer. He gave time for my son to get to know his grandfather. He made a way for my husband to start his own business, when he'd wondered if that would ever happen. And He provided a way for me to work with the kids I loved so much.

The Bible promises that in all things God works for the good of those who love Him. And I believe that's even when the situation seems incredibly difficult or unfair.

From the outside, this time was full of trauma and stress. It certainly was tough. It obviously wasn't the year I'd been expecting. Yet through it all arose incredible windows of opportunity for me, and those I hold most dear. My faith grew as I learned to fully trust in a great and amazing God, whose hand was so clearly and mercifully evident.

TRADING THE "GOOD LIFE" FOR THE "BEST LIFE"

MARGOLYN WOODS

"IT IS GOOD
TO BE TIRED
AND WEARIED
BY THE VAIN
SEARCH
AFTER THE
TRUE GOOD,
THAT WE MAY
STRETCH OUT
OUR ARMS
TO THE
REDEEMER."
—*Blaise Pascal*

But seek ye first the kingdom of God, and his righteousness;

and all these things shall be added unto you.

MATTHEW 6:33

I had a wonderful childhood in Southern California, and life became really exciting for me in college when I was named 1972 "Tournament of Roses" Rose Bowl Queen. During my reign, I appeared on numerous television shows—the Bob Hope Christmas Show, the Carol Burnett Show, the Flip Wilson Show—and starred in the first television commercial for a brand new product called the Polaroid Camera !

After my exciting year in the limelight, I just knew I wanted a career in show business. I got some exciting roles on shows like "Vegas" and I also became the spokesperson for a new product "Rose Milk Skin Care Cream." Things were happening fast. Stars were in my eyes as my acting career seemed to take off.

At a dinner party one evening, I met a well-known film producer. After an exciting year of dating, we were married in a star-studded ceremony. But our joy was short lived. I was lonely, unfulfilled, and disillusioned, and after several years, we divorced.

After about a year, I met Roy, a professional racecar driver. I knew right away that he was marriage material. He wanted to settle down; he wanted children; he was absolutely charming!

After just three-weeks, we ran off to Las Vegas. I hadn't planned on eloping, but Roy's next race was in Le Mans, France and it sounded so romantic to elope and run off to France! So, we flew to Las Vegas and got married on the strip in a little pink chapel . Not exactly what I had hoped for in a wedding, but I had the man of my dreams, and this time I knew it was forever.

Our honeymoon in the south of France was a girl's dream come true with wonderful hotels and incredible meals. We had a storybook romance. I willingly sacrificed my escalating career for the promise of an exciting new life in Oklahoma with my race car driver. And life did, indeed, seem perfect. Our home was an incredible estate called "Out of Bounds," where my daily routine consisted of choosing a menu for the cook, doing a little volunteer work on the side, and playing tennis. For a while, everything was a dream come true. We had everything money could buy. Our lives were filled with wonderful trips, private planes and lots of love. It was a lifestyle I had only read about in romance novels.

But after several years on the racecar circuit with Roy, I was ready to settle down. I thought Roy was ready, too, but when I asked him to give up racing, he said "Someday, but not now." When I brought up having children, I got the same response. When I asked him to at least come home each evening to sit down to dinner with me, he reminded me how lucky I was to have him.

I'm sure that people looking at our lives from the outside must have thought that we had everything. But by this time neither of us was very happy, and I recognized the signs of a marriage in trouble because I'd been there before.

I thought going to church might help. Although my life probably didn't reflect it, I viewed myself a Christian. I grew up going to church. I sang in the choir and was even part of a youth group. Now seemed like a good time to start again. But when I asked Roy to go to church, he just said, "On my golf day?"

During this troubled period, the Hartzog family befriended me. On Sunday mornings, while Roy was off on a racetrack or a golf course, Larry and Gretchen, along with their seven children, came by to pick me up for church. Soon Gretchen graciously allowed me to cry on her shoulder for hours, telling her my heartache. She patiently listened to every word I said. Then she asked me if I had ever asked Jesus Christ to come into my life.

I couldn't believe what I was hearing. With all the time I had spent in church, I had never heard it said that to be a child of God,

I needed to take that first step and ask Jesus Christ into my life.

Gretchen then asked if I would like to say a prayer asking Jesus into my heart. Well, my life sure wasn't working out very well with me in charge, so I agreed and asked Jesus to come into my life. I asked Him to make me into the woman He wanted me to be, and I asked Him to help me with my marriage.

It was if a light came on. I now knew that I had been trying to fill a void in my life that only Jesus could fill. I had thought that accolades, a husband, money, and things would bring me lasting happiness, but they had not.

As I began to study the Bible and spend time in church and in prayer, Roy moved further and further away from me. Finally, because of his infidelity, I felt that I had to leave the marriage. Devastated at my second failure, I moved to Colorado where, with the help of friends, I slowly began to put my life back together.

Knowing how very angry I was with Roy, a friend suggested that I ask God to change my heart towards him. Wow, letting go of my anger was very difficult for me. I felt justified in holding onto it, yet I also strongly desired to please God. So, reluctantly, but honestly, I prayed that God would change my heart toward Roy. In time, with the help of new friends and a busy new life, the pain diminished and my anger slowly faded.

About a year later, there was a knock at my door. There was Roy, standing with suitcase in hand, wanting to start over. The divorce had already gone through, but I let him move back in.

Things went well for a while, and I thought we would be able to work things out. We were starting over in a new town, and he seemed to like Colorado. I was even beginning to trust him again.

But life in the world's fast lane still had a hold on Roy, and one day I came home to a note saying he had left. Once again I was completely shattered. A month later, I found out I was also pregnant. I was devastated. I had two failed marriages, I was thirty-one years old, and now I was going to be a single parent!

For the first two months, I simply felt sorry for myself. Then, I believe that God opened my eyes to the wonderment of having a baby. I started staring into the faces of every baby I saw, wondering if I was carrying a girl or a boy—wondering if my baby was healthy. I got down on my knees and asked God to stay really close to me while I had this baby. I sold my home and moved to Maui, Hawaii, where Roy and I shared a condo as part of our divorce settlement.

The first Sunday after I arrived, I visited a church, and in the church bulletin was an announcement that a childbirth class was starting that evening. That night we went around the room introducing ourselves and sharing why we chose this particular birth class. When my turn arrived, I broke down and told these total strangers my entire life's story. Today, I am so thankful for that group of Christian husbands and wives who literally put their arms around me and helped me through one of the most difficult times in my life.

About six months later, there was another knock at my door. It was Roy again, suitcase in hand, wanting to start over. And boy, were those Christian husbands ready for him! They picked him up to play golf; they took him to play tennis; they invited us to their homes. Roy began to see that these men truly were different. They had a "high" in their lives without drugs or expensive toys, they showed incredible respect for their wives and their families and they selflessly cared about Roy.

Roy began to attend church with me, and one day when our Pastor asked if there was anyone who wanted to give their life over to Jesus Christ Roy asked Jesus into his heart.

If anyone had told me that I would not only forgive him, but that I would fall in love with Roy all over again, I would never have believed them. But with God nothing is impossible. With God as the foundation in our lives, Roy and I now have a wonderful marriage, and there is joy and peace in our home. Our lives are rich with love and happiness. Our priorities have completely changed. Our life goal now is not to have all that the world offers, but to have our children, family, and friends know God as intimately and fully as we know Him. We want to do for others what our church friends did for us—leading us to the life changing love of Jesus.

 A CLEAR CONSCIENCE

KITTY CHAPPELL

Abstain from all appearance of evil.

1 T H E S S A L O N I A N S   5 : 2 2

"IT'S NOT WHO IS RIGHT, BUT WHAT IS RIGHT."

Anonymous

I couldn't believe what I had just heard! "Pardon me?" I asked.

"I said," the department manager repeated slowly, "you could be terminated for your actions."

Minutes earlier, my supervisor had told me that Mr. Brooks wanted to see me in his office—immediately. When I asked why, she had shrugged—yet every eye followed me as I left the room.

Mr. Brooks got right to the point. "Mrs. Chappell, we have reports that you have been observed leaving the hospital cafeteria, clocking in on the time clock, only to reenter the cafeteria and stay longer. Your actions are tantamount to stealing from this facility."

Mr. Brooks' accusation was correct. As a slow eater, I disliked having to rush through my evening meals at the community hospital where I worked the evening shift. We had only thirty minutes in which to get our tray, go through the food line, wait in line at the cash register, find a table, hurriedly eat, and then clock in before rushing back to our departments.

I had recently started clocking in, and instead of returning to my department, I returned to my table for an extra fifteen minutes. I then compensated for staying the extra time by taking only one of my two daily coffee breaks.

I considered myself a conscientious employee. I even gave time in ways not required. Once I accidentally broke a long tape before it was transcribed. Several unhappy doctors had to re-dictate their reports. That weekend, I drove to the hospital and worked undetected at my station for several hours without clocking in. No one knew, of course, but I did. It was my way of making up for the trouble I had caused.

My conscience is clear in every area, I thought. *How can he sit there and call me a thief?*

"Mr. Brooks, I would never steal from anyone," I said, my face burning.

"Time is money," he replied, without expression. "When you steal time from your employer, that is the same as stealing money."

"I understand, " I stammered, "but I've not been stealing time." I then explained how I skipped one of my breaks each day to extend my mealtime, making sure to always take only one break.

"By law we must provide two breaks a day—and you need those breaks," he explained. "You're not the only one who has just thirty minutes for meals. You will need to eat faster or talk less. Hereafter, you will take your breaks, and you will return to your department after clocking in. Is that understood?"

"Yes, Mr. Brooks." I fumed as I walked toward my department. *I wonder who the snitch is who started all of this?*

I made a quick mental rundown of possible suspects. Probably that unfriendly woman from accounting—I've noticed her watching me. Or that grumpy guy from radiology. Whoever it is, they ought to get a life! Didn't they have anything better to do than spy on fellow employees?

Mostly, I worried about what my coworkers would think. I'd tried hard to "walk my talk" as a Christian. And there I was—a Sunday school teacher—accused of thievery!

Detouring into the women's lounge, I splashed cold water on my flushed face. Defensive thoughts popped into my mind as I reached for a paper towel. *How can you just lie down and do nothing to save your reputation? Your friends believe in you. Let them know how insulted you feel—with a humble but martyred air, of course. Refer to your good work ethics and habits. Remind them how often you volunteer to transcribe difficult tapes that others don't want to do. They'll rally to support you. Especially since they do worse things than you do. It won't change anything, but you owe it to them to fight for your reputation.*

That made sense to me. After all, my conscience was clear. Suddenly, I recalled my mother's voice from across the years. "Kitty, the issue is not who is right, but what is right. I don't care who started it, I want it stopped right now!"

Just as I did back then, I argued.

Yes, but it isn't right for me to be accused of something I didn't do!

God's Spirit stepped in and nudged me. *But you did do it.* By not following the rules, I gave a wrong message to others. How could they know I wasn't stealing time? They could only know what they saw. If they saw me do something that really shouldn't be done, they could either question my integrity or be tempted to do the same that I was doing. I knew I needed to set a good example at all times, in all areas.

I wrestled with each line of thinking as I returned to my department. *Should I try to protect my image (and my pride), or would I humiliate myself by assuming responsibility for my actions?*

"What happened?" everyone asked in unison as I entered. They waited for my answer, every eye upon me.

These were my friends, ready to take my side. Didn't I owe them something? Yes, I decided.

"Mr. Brooks accused me of breaking hospital rules by reentering the cafeteria after clocking in at dinnertime and then staying longer."

As expected, my coworkers voiced every objection and presented every justification for my actions that I had already thought of. Squaring my shoulders, I resisted the temptation to avoid my call to accountability and deflected their loyalty by telling them the truth.

"Mr. Brooks was right," I said. "Oh, I didn't think I was actually breaking any rules, just sort of twisting them. I felt justified since I didn't take my second break, but I was wrong. I not only broke the rules, I gave the wrong impression and caused problems by trying to live above the rules."

I heard myself conclude with the statement, "After all, the issue is not who is right but what is right."

LOST ON MOUNT DIABLO

JANICE BRAUN WILLIAMS

For He will command his angels concerning you to guard you in all

your ways; they will lift you up in their hands, so that you will not

strike your foot against a stone.

PSALM 91:11 NIV

"FAITH IS
NOT BEING
SURE OF
WHERE YOU'RE
GOING, BUT
GOING
ANYWAY."

Frederick Buechner

I can see Mount Diablo from my bedroom window, rising out of the early morning clouds like a giant monument to the Almighty. Since the day the flier came in the mail announcing the upcoming trail ride on Mount Diablo, I've looked forward to riding the miles of trails with my equestrian friends.

The day finally arrived. I'm a fifty-seven-year-old grandmother, but was excited as if I were a little kid again. I awoke before the sun came up although the ride didn't start until 3:00 P.M. I listened to the weather report. The temperature was expected to be in the eighties to low nineties. Nonetheless,

I tied a jacket to the back of the saddle. I toyed with the idea of taking a cell phone, but decided against it. After all, I am going to ride Mount Diablo to get away from it all, to experience the bountiful wildlife, and to visit with my friends.

I rode my show horse, GA Desert Sheik, a white Arabian gelding. Sheik and I traveled the show circuit for several years, but this was the first time on Mount Diablo for both of us. In anticipation of a great day, I loaded Sheik into the horse trailer, kissed my husband good-bye, and drove to the appointed location where the rest of the riders waited.

Sheik and I, along with the other horse-and-rider teams, were challenged with rugged trails and fast-running streams. Sheik had never seen water cascading over rocks. He pranced sideways and refused to cross the water, but once the rest of the horses were on the other side, he gave up the fight and plunged through the cold mountain stream.

I was ecstatic, alive with nature.

At the halfway point, the lead rider called for a stop to rest. I dismounted along with the others to take pictures of a sheer granite cliff. It's a spiritual place, like Half Dome in Yosemite. I sensed the enormity of God's creation and thanked Him for His handiwork.

The lead rider informed us there were stragglers. "We'll wait for them," he announced as he walked down the line of horses and riders.

An hour later, he made the decision to ride on, so I volunteered to stay behind to wait for the others. Happily, I found a large boulder to sit on and wave to the departing riders. Sheik whinnied a couple of times and cocked his head as the last horse and rider disappeared around a bend in the trail.

"It's all right, boy, we're waiting for the others," I told him. I allowed Sheik to graze to the end of the reins, and he promptly forgot that we were alone.

I was lost in the beauty. Time seemed to stand still as the sun dipped behind the rock wall. It was then that I realized no other riders were coming. Suddenly the thought of being alone on the mountain after dark sent a shiver down my spine.

Dusk brought four coyotes slinking through the underbrush. They were close enough to catch our scent. My heart began to pound, and I uttered my first prayer of the night.

God, protect us.

The foursome stopped and stared. Sheik raised his head and I heard a grumble rise from deep within his throat. The coyotes understood. They moved away through the thick brush. My eyes filled with tears. I stand amazed that a show horse, unaccustomed to the great outdoors, could command such authority. Looking back now I understand it was God who truly commanded such authority.

I decided that something must have happened to the riders I was waiting for. I mounted up and followed the tracks of the horses that left earlier. I checked my watch in the fading light. Eight o'clock. Within the half hour the last vestiges of daylight were gone. I could no longer see the tracks of the other horses. My heart filled with panic as I recalled a sign near the entrance to the mountain. The park gates were locked at eight o'clock.

A cougar approached from the underbrush. Sheik lifted his head and I felt his body tremble. I felt his muscles bunch beneath my saddle, as if he might take flight. Instead he made that same low grumbling noise in his throat. The cougar was close enough that I could see his eyes. He moved toward us. My breath caught in my throat, and I uttered my second prayer of the night.

God, protect us.

My courageous mount lowered his head and pawed the dirt. I could hardly believe it as I watched the cougar back away and disappear into the night.

"We have to find a way off the mountain, buddy," I said and gave Sheik a gentle thump in the ribs with my boot heel.

The trail narrowed and disappeared up a steep trail. Sheik turned onto it, but seeing no visible signs of horse droppings, I insisted we turn around. Later I learned that this was the way back. Several frustrating hours passed. I called out to someone—anyone who might be looking for me. The temperature on the mountain dropped quickly. I thanked God for reminding me to tie a jacket to my saddle as a heavy mist began to fall. I pondered the thought of sleeping on the mountain. As the cold and damp seeped into my bones, I despaired of ever finding anyone, when suddenly a husband and wife answered my frantic call into the darkness.

I rode toward their voices, but a fence separated us.

"What are you doing out here?" the man asked, shining a flashlight in my face. A woman stood beside him holding a dog by a leash. I can tell by her expression she was as shocked as her husband was to see a woman riding alone, after dark, on Mount Diablo.

"I was riding with friends. Some of them fell behind, and I waited for them while the others returned to the trailer parking area." My lips shivered from fright and cold. "All the gates are locked. I can't find a way off the mountain," I explained.

I checked my watch. Eleven o'clock. I'd been on the mountain alone for hours. My stomach growled from hunger, and Sheik pranced with impatience. He wanted to go home.

"I saw a light over there." The man nodded to a growth of trees. "Maybe they know of a gate that's open." The man took the dog from his wife. At the time, I didn't think anything of it. But when he returned with a bearded, barefoot, hippie-type man, I understood—he probably wanted the dog for protection.

"I hear you're lost," the man said, shining his light in my face. "Where are you supposed to be?"

"On the Danville side of the mountain," I replied.

"That's twenty miles away," he said.

My heart sank, and I began to cry.

"I know where there's a pedestrian gate that isn't locked. It might be big enough for you to get your horse through." The man gave me directions. "Another mile or two down that trail." He shined his flashlight on a narrow path. "Turn right down a steep gully. There's another trail at the bottom. Turn left. I'll be waiting for you."

True to his word, a man I didn't know, a man I feared almost as much as the mountain itself, met me at the gate. I saw his beacon of light flashing in the darkness and reminded myself that angels come in strange packages.

This dear man walked with me to the nearest house. I rang the doorbell and explained my circumstances to the sleepy-eyed man who answered the door. In turn he called the police, who called the park rangers. They told him they were looking for me on the other side of the mountain.

Thirty minutes later a friend of mine came to pick Sheik and me up. When I turned to thank the man who had helped me get off the mountain, he was gone.

All I could do was breathe a simple prayer: *Thank You, God, for protecting us.*

ANYA'S GIFT

RENIE (SZILAK) BURGHARDT

If a son shall ask bread of any of you that is a father, will he give him
a stone? or if he ask a fish, will he for a fish give him a serpent? Or
if he shall ask an egg, will he offer him a scorpion? If ye then, being
evil, know how to give good gifts unto your children: how much more
shall your heavenly Father give the Holy Spirit to them that ask him?

LUKE 11:11-13

"IT IS NOT
HOW MUCH
WE HAVE, BUT
HOW MUCH
WE ENJOY,
THAT MAKES
HAPPINESS."
Charles Spurgeon

My eleventh birthday was just a week away when we arrived in the refugee camp on that bleak and cold November day in 1947. My grandparents, who were raising me, and I had successfully fled the Soviet-occupied communist country, Hungary, with only the clothes on our backs. The refugee camp, called a "Displaced Persons Camp," was in Spittal, Austria.

To frightened, cold, and hungry people like us, the refugee camp was a blessing. We were given warm clothes, our own little cardboard-enclosed space in a barrack, and fed hot cabbage and potato soup. We had so much to be grateful for. I didn't even want to think about my upcoming birthday. After all, we had left our country without any possessions or money. Even if Apa (my grandfather) had managed to flee with a few pengos (Hungarian coins) in his pocket, it wouldn't have done us any good in Austria. So I decided to forget about birthday presents.

My grandmother, the only mother I had ever known, took over my care when my mother died suddenly. I was only a few weeks old at the time. Before the war intensified, my birthdays had been grand celebrations with many cousins in attendance, and lots of gifts of toys, books, and clothes. The cake had always been a dobosh torte, which Anya (my grandmother) prepared herself.

The war changed all of that. My eighth birthday had been the last time I received a purchased gift. Times were already hard, money was scarce, and survival was the primary goal, but my grandparents had managed to sell something so they could buy me a book. It was a wonderful book, too, full of humor and adventure, and I loved it. In fact, *Cilike's Adventures* transported me many times from the harshness of the real world I lived in, to a world of laughter and fun.

Before the refugee camp, thanks to Anya's deft fingers, birthday presents were usually crocheted or knitted items, but there was always a gift. However, there in the refugee camp, I resigned myself to the inevitable. There would be no presents for me that year.

On November 25, when I awoke in our cardboard cubicle, I lay there on my little cot beneath the horsehair blanket and thought about turning eleven. *Why, I was practically a grown-up,* I told myself, *and I would act accordingly when Anya and Apa awoke.* I didn't want them to feel bad because they couldn't give me a present. So I dressed quickly and tiptoed out as quietly as possible. Outside, I ran across the frosty dirt road to the barrack marked "Women's Bathroom and Shower," to wash and comb my hair. I took my time although it was chilly before returning to our cubicle.

"Good morning, Sweetheart. Happy birthday," Apa greeted me as soon as I walked in.

"Thank you. But I'd just as soon forget about birthdays from now on," I replied, squirming in his generous hug.

"You are too young to forget about birthdays," Anya said, taking me in her arms. "Besides, whom would I give this present to if birthdays are to be forgotten?"

"Present?" I looked at her dumbfounded, as she reached into her pocket and pulled something out.

"Happy birthday, Honey. It's not much of a present, but I thought you might enjoy having *Cilike* back on your eleventh birthday," she said, tears welling up in her eyes.

It was my old *Cilike's Adventures* book! "But I thought it was left behind with all our other things," I cried, hugging the book to my chest, tears of joy welling up in my own eyes.

"Well, it almost was. But when we had to leave so quickly in the middle of the night, I grabbed it, along with my prayer book, and stuck it in my pocket. I knew how much you loved that book, and I couldn't bear to leave it behind. Happy birthday, again, Honey. I'm sorry it's not a new book, but I hope you like having it back."

"Oh, thank you, Anya! Having Cilike back means so much to me. So very much," I said, hugging her again, tears streaming down my cheeks. "It's the best birthday present I ever received!" And it truly was, because I realized that day that God had blessed me with a wonderful grandmother, whose love would always see me through.

God had loved me enough to make sure I had a birthday present that year, and even more importantly, He gave me wonderful people to love and care for me during very difficult times. As much as I depended on my grandparents, I discovered my relationship with God would prove Him forever the most dependable person I could ever trust.

COVERED BY HIS FEATHERS

JOAN CLAYTON

He will cover you with his feathers, and

under his wings you will find refuge.

PSALM 91:4 NIV

"HOPE IS THE THING WITH FEATHERS THAT PERCHES IN THE SOUL."

Emily Dickinson

I thought my heart would break. The misunderstanding I'd had with a loved one threatened to shatter the whole family. Communication all but disappeared, and tempers were lit with short fuses. There was no peace.

"Let it go!" my husband repeatedly told me. "There's not any sense in making yourself sick over it. We have prayed about it, and that's all we can do."

Emmitt's faith had always sustained us throughout our thirty years of marriage. He'd been the strong one when the storms of life blew against our windowpanes of love.

Somehow in this crisis I couldn't seem to keep from replaying my "if-onlys" and "what-ifs."

One particular night, I tossed and turned into the wee hours. *How can he sleep like that?* I wondered, watching Emmitt. The minute his head hits the pillow, he starts snoring!

I finally drifted off to sleep, but when I awoke the next morning, total peace had enveloped me. It was astounding!

The pressure and anxiety I had experienced the night before somehow vanished. I even tried to worry and found I couldn't. I tried to be upset. It just did not happen. How strange! As far as I knew, nothing in the circumstances had changed. The situation was the same, but I had a blanket of peace covering my heart.

"I don't know how to tell you this," I told my loving husband, "but I don't have anxiety anymore. I know that God is in control, and all of a sudden, I can completely let go of it. I don't understand it."

"Honey," Emmitt held me close and whispered, "I was praying last night about the situation, and as I drifted off to sleep, the most wonderful thing happened. Maybe it was a dream. I don't know. But I do know what I saw. From far in the distance, this beautiful angel dressed in white came to my side of the bed. He was the most beautiful creature. I can even see it now—I'm going to have to paint that picture someday."

(Emmitt is an artist.)

"When the angel stopped at my side of the bed, he covered us with his beautiful white feathers. They unfolded and rippled over us, covering us completely."

Emmitt's voice began to break, and tears trickled down his cheeks. This experience touched his heart, and I cried happy tears too. Emmitt's faith-filled prayer had covered everything, including me.

I did not know God's Word very well at that time, but imagine my joy and surprise when we arrived at church that Sunday morning. While waiting for the services to begin, I randomly opened my Bible and gasped!

My eyes gazed upon this passage: "He will cover you with his feathers, and under his wings you will find refuge" (Psalm 91:4).

That day marked a turning point in my prayer life. It is many years later, yet Emmitt and I still remember the day our prayers took a "U-turn" and the lesson we learned: "God is our refuge in every situation."

$\mathscr{T}$HE APPEARANCE OF ANGELS

ELIZABETH BEZANT

Give as freely as you have received.

MATTHEW 10:8 NLT

"GREAT OPPORTUNITIES TO HELP OTHERS SELDOM COME, BUT SMALL ONES SURROUND US EVERY DAY."

Sally Koch

Thirteen years had passed since my emigration from England, and as the plane touched down at Heathrow, years of long forgotten memories cascaded through me. So many thoughts, feelings, and senses flooded my mind—emotions I had blocked out to stave off homesickness suddenly bubbled to the surface.

Outside the metal cocoon of our jetliner, the world was waking up. The roads were beginning to fill, and the airport was coming alive with people arriving for their early flights.

I felt strangely liberated to travel on my own, but at the same time, I felt the subtle ache caused by leaving my young family behind. I had returned to my homeland more than once over the years, but this was the first time I would step off the plane alone. *Could my family really manage without me?* I wondered. *Had I left them prepared for everything that might happen in my absence? What had I forgotten to do? What message had I forgotten to pass on?*

They were standard concerns of a mother and wife I guess, but four weeks was a long time to be away.

Still, our time apart was for a good reason. My mother needed me to help her as she recuperated from a life-threatening illness. What better reason could there be than that? After all, how many times in our lives do we get a chance to repay, at least in part, the generosity, time, and selflessness our parents bestowed on us?

For some of us there are only a few times throughout life when the roles of parents and children are reversed. Yet, I had been given the opportunity, and I did not want to pass it up. I wanted to care for my mother as she had so many times cared for me.

No requests were made for me to make the journey. No off-hand queries on the possibilities. No mentions on how useful I could be if only I was with her. The offer had been mine, the choice had been mine, and I was grateful that my mother had accepted.

Thankfully, my husband, while he did not fully understand

the bond between my mother and me, did accept its existence. So did my children, although the parting looks on the faces of my four- and eight-year-olds nearly tore me apart.

The last few days had been hectic, but here I was, five days and twelve thousand miles later, in Heathrow.

During those five days, I had been swamped with the well wishes and generosity of all kinds of people. Friends that I hadn't known for more than several months offered to help with the care of my two girls before and after school. Others reorganized their school holidays to care for my children during the long hours of my husband's new job.

I read once that angels come in all shapes and sizes, all colors and creeds, all ages and all lifestyles. Where they come from no longer concerns me, but how they always turn up when I need them most always surprises me. Many times I wonder if I will ever be able to repay their kindness or whether, if our roles were reversed, I would do the same.

As I walked out of the airport lounge, I saw my brother for the first time in years, and all my other thoughts were forgotten. It was not until the next day when Mum arrived home from the hospital that the thoughts reentered my mind. Standing there, temporarily frail and dependent, she clutched my hand, holding it as if she never wanted to let go. Sitting down on the sofa, her tired eyes glanced around at the reassuring familiarity of her home before they returned to me.

"I prayed that you would come," she said quietly. "I needed you here beside me, but I never believed you could come."

And for a moment, I saw in her eyes a look of acceptance that prayers can come true. A look that said, "I needed you and you appeared." And in that moment, I too felt that I had wings.

PACKAGE DEAL

DIANE DWYER

Let us hold unswervingly to the hope we profess,

for he who promised is faithful.

HEBREWS 10:23 NIV

On that overcast October afternoon, I looked plenty pitiful. Standing at the barn beside my beat-up little travel trailer, with no car to pull it; my horse, with no trailer to transport him; and four trusting dogs, expecting me to feed them—I presented a sad sight. But we came as a package deal, and that day, there were no demands for package deals.

In the past I had asked God to lead me, and I tried to follow. But now doubts piled on top of one another; I had lost my job. I questioned in my mind, *Lord, have I chosen the wrong line of work?*

I had been living in a furnished mobile home on a large farm where I trained and cared for thirty horses and everything

"THIS ABOVE ALL: TO THINE OWN SELF BE TRUE, AND IT MUST FOLLOW, AS THE NIGHT THE DAY, THOU CANST NOT BE FALSE TO ANY MAN."

William Shakespeare
Hamlet

else that goes with the job. I love working with horses—have devoted forty-five years to it—but the work had become too hard for one person to handle.

I dutifully wrote my employer a thirty-day notice of resignation. Without warning harsh words flew when I delivered the message, ending with a notice, "You are leaving now!"

Leaving! Where in the world will I go? I had counted on using those thirty days to train someone to take my place and to locate a new home for my "family." With my two sons grown and living away, that family now consisted of my horse and four dogs—almost as precious to me as my children.

My furry family stood there looking to me for answers: Princely Swift Viking, my dark brown appendix quarter horse with the nickname of Vi-Guy; three Bassets—Lovey, a retired show dog; Lamar and Andrew, foster children I adopted from the Basset Hound Rescue; and Rudy, the precious miniature Dachshund I saved from almost certain euthanasia, having brought him home in a borrowed doggy wheelchair.

"Don't you worry, Vi-Guy," I said, stroking the white star on his forehead. "We'll find you a wonderful pasture with a stream and a nice warm barn. Just you wait and see."

"And you guys," I said, kneeling down to hug the canine quartet surrounding me, demanding attention. "We'll be okay. I know we will."

But on the inside, I wondered if, when, and how I could fulfill those promises.

I faced some serious soul-searching. I knew the questions I'd get from my grown children: "Mother, why don't you get a real job? One that pays better. One with some security."

I'd heard it all before, even from friends. It all ran through my mind as I stood there in a daze. My plants and memorabilia—where will I put them? Where will I hang my clothes? And what about my family? "Lord," I cried out. "I need Your help here, real bad."

I phoned the teacher of my new Bible study class and shared my plight. "I'll be over in the morning to get your plants and care for them," she offered. "How else can I help?"

A few minutes later, a member of the class called. "Tomorrow I'll canvass stores in town for cardboard boxes to help you pack," she said.

Around 9:30 that night a young man who boarded his horse at the farm, knocked on my door. His mother was with him. "We want to help you," she said. "We know what it's like to be without a home. Ours burned down earlier this year. You can park your trailer in our yard until you decide what to do."

The next morning, another boarder said, "I have an empty pasture. I'll keep Vi-Guy for you."

Still another one heard that conversation. "Vi-Guy will be lonely all by himself. I'll take my two donkeys out there to keep him company."

I couldn't believe the kindness of these people! Tears threatened to spill down my face when yet another boarder said, "Let me take your dogs to the kennel for a few days while you relocate. I'll pay the bill."

In spite of the rain that lasted days, I managed to get my meager belongings into storage and prepare for the move. The hardest part was saying good-bye to Vi-Guy, knowing I couldn't see him often. Wearing a downcast face he leaned over, nudged me, and closed his eyes for my kiss. "I'll come get you, Vi," I said, giving him one last hug, "just as soon as I can."

Through it all, every Sunday I attended the Bible study class and reported on my progress, or lack of it. The members encouraged me and prayed regularly for me. And during those three months, I had many heart-to-heart talks with myself and with the Lord.

In one of our conversations I prayed, *Lord, You know how much I love horses and being outdoors. But if I'm supposed to be doing something else, please lead me to it.* Then I added, *But, Lord, if I'm in the right field, please let me know it without a shadow of a doubt.*

Our entire church embarked on a forty-day study on finding your God-given purpose in life. It was exactly what I needed. One day I felt the Lord say to me, "Be true to yourself, Diane."

But what is my true self? I wondered. Then I answered my own question. My true self needs little in the way of "stuff." I need only food to eat and a safe place to sleep, friends who love me, and animals who need me.

My true self loves horses. From the time I was a nine-year-old I have been a horse-crazy child. I've never gotten over it. I even love barns—the warmth and the way light plays through the beams, changing throughout the day. I like the smell of fresh sawdust and the feel of breezes blowing through the wide center aisle. I like the welcome I receive in the mornings when every horse puts his head over the front of the stall, waiting for a word—and breakfast—from me. I like the night sounds as the horses whinny to one another and the cows out in the pasture low softly.

And I'm good with animals. They love me. Who else serves them their hay with the words, "Here is your salad course. What dressing would you like?" (They always choose "ranch.") After their entrée of oats, often they're offered dessert from the apple chunks in my pocket.

I enjoy training and grooming horses. They are my friends, each with his own personality. When they are all settled in for the night, it reminds me of that satisfied feeling when my boys were little and safely tucked in after a full day of play. Besides, where else would I be considered Queen of the Castle, or in this case, the barn? I've held "real" jobs, as my sons call them, but they just weren't me. I knew now that giving up the work I love was unthinkable. I realized my children and friends have my interests at heart and I love them for it.

Early one December morning, in my jacket pocket I felt a scrap of paper that number I've hesitated to call all these weeks. An inner voice said, "It's time to call it, Diane." Vickie Mead answered. "Why don't you come on over and talk with Brett?" she said.

"I'll be right there," I said, and by 8:30 I was turning into the entrance of picturesque Mountain Creek Ranch. I followed the gravel driveway as it curved around in front of the white-frame main house to reveal, amid the acreage in back, a beautiful barn surrounded by pastures with grazing horses and cattle, spectacular scenery, and even a mountain in the background.

A tour of the barn showed sixteen stalls (one of them empty), a bunkhouse, kitchen, shower facilities, and even an office—all needing someone to use them. *The answer to my prayers!* My mind raced. *Dare I hope?*

Brett Mead asked, "How soon can you be packed?"

"Give me a couple hours," I answered.

"I'll bring the truck over to get you."

By noon my little trailer was snuggled against the side of that barn with a gorgeous view of wooded hills and the mountain. Soon the dogs were exploring their new farm.

"Let's go get your horse," Brett said and off we drove, the horse trailer bouncing along behind us.

When Vi-Guy heard us coming, his head sprang up, and he beat us to the gate. "I told you I was coming back, Vi," I said hugging his neck and kissing his nose. "Just wait until you see our new home!"

When we reached Mountain Creek, I put him in the paddock so he could look around and meet the other horses. Right away he found the creek and played in it like a child on his first day of summer vacation.

It's springtime now—a bright, warm afternoon. Birds sing their little hearts out, busy building nests. With their cheerful background music, I'm eating supper outside. Nearby, Vi-Guy munches grass and the "boys" play at my feet. My eyes rest on the peaceful scene of rolling pasture edged with trees sporting new green leaves, and beyond that—a sunset's purple haze silhouettes Long Mountain.

I couldn't be more content. For this is the real me. And I believe this is exactly where God wants me to be at this moment in time.

Do I have any guarantees about tomorrow? No. But I'm confident that God knows and cares about my welfare. And that is enough.

So take another look. You'll see one happy camper. Make that six happy campers—Vi-Guy, Lovey, Andrew, Lamar, Rudy—and me.

ORGIVE? WHO, ME?

SUZANNAH WILLINGHAM

Bear with each other and forgive whatever grievances you may have against one another. Forgive as the Lord forgave you.

C O L O S S I A N S 3 : 1 3 N I V

"FORGIVENESS IS A FUNNY THING— IT WARMS THE HEART AND COOLS THE STING."
William Arthur Ward

I knew before my wedding that my relationship with my mother-in-law was likely going to be a tightrope walk. The first clue came when the search for my wedding dress quickly became more about what she would wear. Long after I had ruled out the few bridal gowns in a tiny boutique, she continued to slowly peruse the size eight chiffons—dresses not quite her size. It took every ounce of patience I possessed to keep from screaming, "This is about me, not you!" Little did I realize at the time, my patience was about to experience a growth spurt born of necessity.

After the wedding, it didn't take long to discover my mother-in-law had all sorts of unwritten rules about all sorts of things. Only visits to her house counted as visits. If she came to our house, that wasn't a "visit." Later, when we had children, they had to visit her one at a time and only a stay of at least three days qualified as a visit. If she gave me money to buy things for the children, I had to buy what she stipulated, not what they needed. And a telephone call from me was not sufficient as an invitation to our home or an event. Only a paper invitation would do. The list went on and on, and I think you can see that keeping my mother-in-law happy was a high-maintenance job!

Over the years, interpreting and anticipating all these unwritten rules became extremely tedious. Sometimes they applied and sometimes they did not. Occasionally there was an unexpected caveat to a rule just when I thought I had mastered it. At some point, I finally lost my cool and stopped playing the game. The battles escalated from there.

I had always suspected I was the enemy in my mother-in-law's eyes. After all, I had corrupted her only son, tempting him into, of all things, marriage! But when I refused to play her games, I really became a target. Criticism was constant when she was near. Nothing pleased her. Eventually, we hit an impasse that couldn't be navigated. For more than a year, she refused to see us.

Finally, she wrote a letter asking for a meeting on neutral

ground. If I'd known the reason for the meeting, I would never have attended. For more than an hour, she bombarded me with verbal missiles. She wounded me on many levels, recalling the pain of our years of infertility and questioning if our children were really my husband's. She brought up numerous incidents where I had offended her, most of which were manufactured in her mind, or occasions where I recalled the conversation to be far different than she portrayed. The venom of her hatred and resentment of me poured forth in torrents while my husband and I sat, mouths agape.

When her assault slowed, we made a move to leave. As we parted, she stated with quivering chin that she hoped to see us someday in a happier place. Casting a sidelong glance at me, it was clear she was implying a question about my admission to heaven, that happier place in her mind. She benignly handed us a bag of apples, as if the visit had been cordial. My husband and I sat shell-shocked in the car for long moments. At last he whispered, "I never knew she disliked you so much."

For months afterwards, I was consumed with anger. How dare she talk to me like that? She was horrible, not worthy of our love. I took long walks and cried out to God about the injustice of her words and the pain they caused me. I rehearsed awful things I wanted to say to her. I demanded that God strike her down and humble her for her offense to me. Gradually, I

began to hear the word God whispered to me over my tirade—
forgive. At first, I refused to hear. It became louder—
FORGIVE!

Surely not, Lord! How can You ask me to forgive her when she is the offender?

Calmly He replied, *She's My child, too. Just as you hurt, she hurts...forgive.*

For weeks, I stubbornly refused. Why should I forgive her when she had never asked for forgiveness? I argued with God that He was mistaken to request this of me. Yet, the voice persisted. *FORGIVE.* Finally, one day in desperation, weary with my load of anger, I cried out to God, *Why? Why should I forgive?* In a whisper of that still, small voice the reply came, *Because I forgive you. Because I loved you and the world so much, I gave Myself so that you might be forgiven.* I melted before the sinless One, asked Him to forgive me, and then...I forgave her. Peace flooded my body like a cleansing stream. All the anger washed away as I realized the power of the gifts—salvation and forgiveness—both freely given.

The path to a restored relationship with my mother-in-law was a long journey. But worth every purposeful step. Sure we had our ups and downs, but God's gift of forgiveness made the journey possible. Today I can greet her with a hug, a smile, and an "I love you," and there is no pretense in any of them.

Looking back I am profoundly thankful for the loving support of my husband and the gentle nudges from my Heavenly Father to reach out beyond my comfort level. I now celebrate a warm relationship with a very special lady, my mother-in-law, and all of it is possible because barriers were broken down by the amazing power of God's mercy and forgiveness.

BE STILL WITH GOD

NANCY B. GIBBS

Be still, and know that I am God.

PSALM 46:10 NIV

"REMEMBER THAT EVERYTHING HAS GOD'S FINGERS ON IT."

Richard Carlson

All day long, I had been very busy. Picking up trash, cleaning bathrooms, and scrubbing floors had been my agenda for the day. My grown children were coming home for the weekend. I went grocery shopping and prepared for a barbeque supper, complete with ribs and chicken. I wanted everything to be perfect.

Suddenly, it dawned on me that I was dog-tired. I simply couldn't work as long as I could when I was younger. "I've got to rest for a minute," I told my husband, Roy, as I collapsed into my favorite rocking chair. Music was playing, my dog and cat were chasing each other, and the telephone rang.

A scripture from the Psalms popped into my mind: "Be still, and know that I am God" (Psalm 46:10 NIV).

I realized that I hadn't spent much time in prayer that day. Was I too busy to even utter a simple word of thanks to God? Suddenly, the thought of my beautiful patio came to mind. *I can be quiet out there,* I thought. I longed for a few minutes alone with my Savior.

Roy and I had invested a great deal of time and work into the patio that Spring. The flowers and hanging baskets were breathtaking. It was definitely a heavenly place of rest and tranquility. *If I can't be still with God in that environment, I can't be still with Him anywhere,* I thought. While Roy talked on the telephone, I slipped out the backdoor and sat down on my favorite patio chair. I closed my eyes and began to pray, while counting my many blessings.

A bird flew by me, chirping and singing. It interrupted my thoughts, landing on the bird feeder and I watched as it began to eat its dinner. After a few minutes it flew away, singing another song.

I closed my eyes again. A gust of wind blew, causing my wind chimes to dance. They made a joyful sound, but again I lost my concentration on God. I squirmed and wiggled in my chair. I looked up toward the blue sky and saw the clouds moving slowly toward the horizon. The wind died down. My wind chimes finally became quiet.

Again, I bowed in prayer. The honking of a car horn almost

caused me to jump out of my skin. A neighbor driving down the street, waved at me and smiled. I waved back, happy that he cared enough to greet me. I quickly tried once again to settle down, repeating the familiar verse in my mind: "Be still, and know that I am God."

"I'm trying, God. I really am." I whispered. "But You've got to help me here."

The backdoor opened. My husband walked outside. "I love you," he said. "I was wondering where you were." I chuckled as he came over and kissed me, then he turned around and went back inside. He had wanted to check on me and to know that I was all right.

"Where's my quiet time?" I asked God. My heart began to flutter. There was no pain, only a brief sign of life inside of me. *This is impossible,* I thought. There's no time to be still and to know that God is with me. There's too much going on in the world, and entirely too much activity all around me.

"I'm trying, Lord. I really am," I remembered saying. Then I realized that He had been with me the entire time that I spent seeking Him. Unfortunately, I had been too blind to see the blessings He sent my way even as I spent quiet time with Him.

Suddenly it dawned on me. God was speaking to me the entire time that I was attempting to be still. "Thank You for the joy of music," I remembered saying, as I began my quiet time.

He sent a sparrow to lighten my life with song. "Thank You for the comfortable world You created for me, Lord." He sent a gentle breeze. "Thank You for my friends." He sent a neighbor to greet me. "And thank You for my family, God." He sent my sweetheart to offer his sincere sentiments of love. And when I thanked God for the gift of life, He caused my heart to flutter. As I was trying to count my blessings, God was busy multiplying them.

I had looked at the events around me as interruptions, but God sent them as extra-special blessings. I laughed when I realized that sometimes being still also means simply looking, praying, and rejoicing in His creation.

CONNECTING WITH KYOKO

LANITA BRADLEY BOYD

Then shall he give the rain of thy seed, that thou shalt sow the ground withal; and bread of the increase of the earth, and it shall be fat and plenteous: in that day shall thy cattle feed in large pastures.

ISAIAH 30:23

> "WHEN YOU HAVE A HEART FOR GOD, YOU HAVE A HEART FOR MINISTRY. THE TWO GO HAND IN HAND."
>
> *Jill Briscoe*

On a bright July morning, I scooped up my daughter's workbooks she'd left lying on the kitchen counter and hid them in the guest room, since my friends were coming at 8:30 for our weekly Bible study. Eventually everyone left around 10:00, and I was eager to get to work in my home office. I'd taken the month of June off and had told my boss I'd be back to work in July. As I walked the last Bible study participant to her car, I saw a petite Japanese woman park in my neighbor's driveway and start up the front walk.

I spoke to her: "Are you here for Mrs. Ney? I believe she's out of town." (My polite effort to get her to leave.)

She said, "I'll just ring the bell to be sure."

I went back in the house, thinking that this must be the lady Margaret helps with her English, and that really, I should offer to help her today since Margaret was out of town. However, I resisted this idea firmly and poured a cup of coffee to take upstairs as I went to work.

Hesitating, I stood at the bottom of the stairs. I remembered what I'd taught in our Sunday women's class just that month: When the Spirit leads, don't resist. I'd told my boss I'd get started right after my Bible study, I reasoned. (I was still resisting.)

Timidly I looked out the door, assuming the woman would be gone by now. Surely I'd dawdled long enough! But there she was, kneeling on the porch as she wrote a note to leave for Margaret.

Oh, well, I thought. *Here goes.* And I walked across the street, coffee cup in hand, and introduced myself to Kyoko.

"Since Mrs. Ney is gone, would you like to study English with me?" I asked, of course, hoping she'd say no.

"Really?" she responded. "That would be great!" So we walked back across the street together.

I explained to her that I already helped a Ukrainian woman

with her English, so I had some experience. As we entered the front hall, I said, "The materials we use are from the Bible. We read Bible stories and talk about them."

She stopped short, her eyes wide with astonishment. "The Bible!" she exclaimed. "I have been looking for someone to study the Bible with me!"

I was speechless. All I could do was think, *Well, Holy Spirit, You did know what I was supposed to do! I am so glad that I quit resisting Your leading!*

I told her I would gladly teach her from the Bible and showed her mine, which was still lying on the table. She'd never seen one, so I explained the two testaments and its general organization. She asked intelligent questions, such as whether the Old or New Testament was more important, and if she needed to buy a Bible for our study. I assured her that she didn't, and told her I'd get her the workbook that we used. Actually, I didn't have extras, but my daughter did—right there in the bag I'd stashed in the guest room! I produced the workbook, and we started right away.

She said she had a friend in Japan who had been studying the Bible. She had written Kyoko to tell her she thought she would like it very much. "She is not a Christian," Kyoko said, "but she says the Christian life is a very good way to live."

I found that Kyoko too, was very concerned about a good

way to live. She was conscientious and devoted to our weekly studies while continuing her English lessons across the street. We studied the workbooks based on Luke and Acts together, and she absorbed not only the English but also the spiritual concepts. We talked on many topics and became much closer as we studied together. Once, when I told her of some events in my own life, she responded, "The Spirit must have led you to be there for me that first day!"

In May Kyoko returned to live in Japan. I helped her contact a Christian missionary who teaches a Bible study within traveling distance of her home. She asked me, "Is it all right for me to go to their study? I do not want to be a Christian; I do not plan to be baptized." "Of course," I told her, "it would be fine," and encouraged her to go.

I often think of that time, now almost a year ago: I didn't plan to go across the street and offer to help. I didn't plan to obligate myself for any more activities. But with the Holy Spirit's leading, I did, and the rewards have been boundless.

And who knows, with the prompting of the Holy Spirit I'm trusting that Kyoko's plans will change as well!

A PRAYER FOR WINGS

SHAE COOKE

A man who has friends must himself be friendly, but there is
a friend who sticks closer than a brother.

PROVERBS 18:24 NKJV

As a five-year-old child, I prayed daily to Jesus for a pair of wings. My grandmother used to read stories to me about angels, and I imagined them with glowing wings.

Oh, how wonderful it would be if You could give me wings, Jesus, I prayed. Every night I knelt by my bed and prayed for wings—sparkling, translucent wings that would fly me wherever I wanted to go. Each morning, I examined myself in the mirror. Not even a sprout, a bud, or even the smallest stub of a wing appeared.

Why, Jesus, oh, why won't You answer me? That evening at my bedside, I received a reply.

He said, *"No wings...."*

"GOD ANSWERS ALL OUR PRAYERS. SOMETIMES THE ANSWER IS YES. SOMETIMES THE ANSWER IS NO. SOMETIMES THE ANSWER IS, YOU'VE GOT TO BE KIDDING!"

Jimmy Carter

I cried, stomped my feet, and held my breath, hoping He would change His mind, but Jesus again said, *"...no wings."*

Thirty-five wingless years later, I attended a Christmas pageant at my son's school. The cast reenacted the manger scene—the birth of Christ. As the concert began, several small children dressed as angels sauntered warily onstage. They wore lily-white robes, and bouncing gold halos crowned their heads. Their huge wings almost overpowered their small frames. When they filed toward the manger, one of the angels tripped over one wing belonging to the angel in front of him. As the first angel fell, the others followed like a line of neatly stacked dominoes. Within moments, mayhem erupted. One child cried and the rest followed suit. The children tried to get up on their own. Every time they succeeded, they fell right back down again.

Mortified, the children struggled as the audience laughed hysterically. Instead of a holy scene, it looked like a holy mess; a coyote raiding a chicken coop would have created less havoc! Bent and broken wings and feathers flew everywhere. The well-intentioned costume designers had tried to please the cast and audience; however, they didn't consider the effects of these feathery annoyances.

Shortly after the concert, it dawned on me that had God answered my childhood prayer for literal wings, my life could have resembled that scene onstage. He knew that if I suddenly sprouted a true set of wings, my life would have been awkward, if not downright embarrassing! I laughed as I thought of myself with wings. How would I drive a car, put on a dress, or what if I caught the wings in a revolving door?

At forty-something, I trust completely that He knows best. He says no for a reason—and sometimes we just have to wait thirty-five years to find out why.

Sometimes I still have childish wishes. When things don't go the way I would have hoped...I still pout occasionally. But without a doubt I always maintain a certain knowing that God has my best interests at heart, and I thank Him.

EAVEN SENT

RENIE (SZILAK) BURGHARDT

But if we are living in the light of God's presence, just as Christ
does, then we have wonderful fellowship and joy with each other.

1 JOHN 1:7 TLB

"A FAITHFUL
FRIEND IS A
STURDY
SHELTER; HE
WHO FINDS
ONE FINDS A
TREASURE."

Sirach 6:14

I've been thinking about friendship, and the unexplainable
phenomenon it is. Why do we become friends with some
people, and not others? Why do some people have the ability
to touch our lives, and even inspire us to be our best? To have
a friend who can do that is a real blessing.

When I moved from the city to a beautiful, hilly rural area
in the1980s, I was a woman in mid-life, following her dream. I
looked forward to life in the country, where my closest
neighbors would be the wild animals and birds living in the
woods surrounding my house. Soon after my arrival, I also
added some farm animals to my menagerie of two former city
dogs and cats. A goat, chickens, ducks, geese, and turkeys

cackled, quacked, gobbled, and nibbled happily in my yard.

Yet, with all the delightful new company that surrounded me, something was missing. Or I should say someone was missing. I didn't have a close friend, someone in whom I could confide, like the old childhood friends I left behind in the city. I longed to find just one good friend in my new life I had embarked upon, but how? I had known my old set of friends since high school. We had grown up together, matured together, and stood by each other through thick and thin. I was fifty, and worried that perhaps making new friends now would be more difficult.

Then one day, I was leafing through a writer's magazine at the newsstand in town, trying to decide if it had any good articles that would interest me. Suddenly, an older woman with auburn hair, sparkling brown eyes, and a friendly smile came bouncing up the aisle, stopping right next to me. She looked at the magazine I was holding.

"Hi," she said, smiling at me. "Are you interested in writing?"

"Well, yes, I am," I replied.

"So am I," she continued. "By the way, I'm Garnet, and my husband and I just moved back here after being away for quite a few years. He retired from practicing law, and I'm a retired teacher, and I hope to do some writing in the near future. You must be new around here. I don't believe I've ever seen you before."

"Yes, I am kind of new. I live ten miles outside of town, and I moved here from Ohio recently. I hope to do some writing in the near future as well," I told her, "and my name is Renie."

"Nice to meet you, Renie," she said, "You know, this store has a small section where folks can sit and have coffee and a snack or something. Let's get better acquainted over a cup of coffee." By the time we left, we had become friends.

That's how it all began, back in the summer of 1987. Garnet, it turned out, was sixty-six years old at the time; I was fifty. The difference in our ages didn't seem to matter one bit, for Garnet is, and always will be, young at heart.

The year 2003 marks the sixteenth year of our friendship. Garnet is now almost eighty-three, and I am the age she was when we first met. Over the years, we've shared sadness and joy. When Garnet's beloved husband, Glen, passed away nine years ago, I did everything I could to help her bear her sorrow. She has always been there when I needed her. She calls or e-mails me every evening to make sure all is well. I do the same for her every morning.

One evening recently, I didn't hear from Garnet, so I picked up the phone to call her to make sure she was well, and discovered my phone was out of order. Of course, I was worried, but there was nothing I could do about it that night—I lived ten miles from town, and didn't like driving in the dark. I went to bed with an uneasy feeling, and was unable to fall asleep.

About eleven o'clock, the dogs began to bark furiously, as if someone was coming. Frightened, I got up and looked out my window, and was relieved to see a sheriff deputy's car driving in. He came to my door.

"Hello, ma'am. Your friend Garnet is very worried about you. Since she couldn't get you on the phone, she finally called us to come out and check on you. Is everything all right?"

"Oh, well, bless her heart, that was so very nice of her, officer," I replied, relieved and touched by Garnet's concern. "Yes, I'm all right, but my phone is not. Could you tell Garnet to call the phone company and report it for me? And please thank her for her kindness. I'm very fortunate to have a friend like her."

If I ever feel lonely, just want to talk, don't feel like eating alone, or want to hike around and look for wildflowers, my dear friend Garnet is always willing to join me, and her wise counsel throughout life's ups and downs has often helped me make good decisions.

I read somewhere that we make our own friends when we are young, but the friends who come to us later in life are heaven sent. I know this is true, for God blessed my life when He sent my dear friend Garnet to me.

DREAM COME TRUE

OSEOLA McCARTY

He who gathers money little by little makes it grow.

PROVERBS 13:11 NIV

"IT IS ONE OF THE MOST BEAUTIFUL COMPENSATIONS OF LIFE THAT NO MAN CAN SINCERELY TRY TO HELP ANOTHER WITHOUT HELPING HIMSELF."

Ralph Waldo Emerson

I was born on a farm in Choctaw County, Mississippi, ninety-two years ago. I grew up there with my mama, grandmother, and aunt. We raised corn, peas, and potatoes, and we used to wash our clothes outside in a big black cast-iron pot.

When we moved to Hattiesburg in 1916, we brought that pot with us. It was our pot of treasure, because it helped us make a living. In it my grandmother and mother did washing for white folks. They carried the water from a hydrant and filled up the big pot, which set on a bench in the backyard of our little frame house. Mama boiled the clothes—she wouldn't scrub them—then rinsed and hung them on the line with wooden clothespins.

When I was a very little girl, I would try to throw clothes in the pot. I thought I was helping, but really I was just making a mess. My great-grandmother would call over to Mama: "Lucy, let that child wash the smaller pieces, the socks and things!" So Mama let me stand on a wooden box and put some socks into the water. That was how it all began.

I loved to wash and iron. When I started school, I would wash my own clothes on Saturday mornings, standing on my box so I could reach the pot. Then I took my box out to the clothesline so I could reach up and hang my clean clothes out to dry in the morning sun. In the evening, I would heat up Mama's heavy old iron on the cookstove and iron my clothes while standing on that box. All my clothes were ready for the next week by the time I went to bed on Saturday night.

I loved school and every one of my teachers, especially Mrs. White. I was about ten years old when she said to me one day, "Oseola, come up here to my desk." She talked to me in a low whisper so no one else could hear: "Oseola, who irons your clothes?"

"I do."

"You do? Oh, my. Well, I've got a linen dress I'd like you to iron. What do you charge?"

"Ten cents," I replied. But when I returned the dress, freshly washed and ironed, she paid me a quarter. As time went on one person told another about my washing and ironing, and the work just seemed to come. The more I did, the more money I made.

Some children in the household where my grandmother worked had discarded a doll and buggy, so Grandma brought them home for me. I started putting my dimes, nickels, and quarters under the pink lining of the doll buggy.

When I was twelve my aunt took sick, so I had to drop out of the sixth grade to look after her. I was sad to miss out on learning, but it felt good to help my aunt. The next year my classmates had moved on, and because I had fallen so far behind, I never went back to school. Instead, I kept washing, ironing, and tucking money under the pink lining of that buggy.

I was the one who went around to the grocer and the milkman to pay our bills each month. One day I passed the bank and it occurred to me that I should keep my money there. I took in all my coins and dumped them on the counter—I can't tell you how much I had for sure, maybe five dollars. The teller put my money away in a checking account, and every month, when I paid the bills, I dropped off more coins at the bank. All, that is, except for what I put in the collection plate at the Friendship Baptist Church. No one taught me to do that. It just seemed right to give God back something of what He had given me.

The years passed. The Depression came when I was in my twenties, but I continued to take on jobs washing. I still used the old cast-iron pot, but now I didn't need to stand on a box. I loved to work. I always asked the Lord to give me health, strength, and some work to do. Over the years He did just that.

Some people today have financial advisors to tell them how to save their money. Some people want more of this or more of that to make them happy, and they just can't get enough. Well, the Lord portioned out the good things in life to me just fine. I never needed more than I had.

I made a rule that I would always give to my church and once a year I made a payment on my insurance and my burial plot. Every month I paid my water, electricity, and gas bills, and set aside a certain amount for groceries and everyday needs. Over the years, God taught me to spend money on the things I needed and to save the rest. It must have been Him because no one else was there to show me!

One day, when I went to the bank to make a deposit, the teller said, "Oseola, if you put your money in a savings account, you'll get some interest on that money."

"Yes, ma'am. When can I do it?" I asked.

"You can do it now," she said. And I did.

Then on another visit one of the people at the bank said to me, "Oseola, you ought to put your money in CDs and build up more money."

And I said, "Yes, ma'am. When can I do that?"

And she said, "Right now." So I did, and my money just kept on building. I would deposit sometimes twenty dollars a month, sometimes fifteen dollars. I only went to the bank to put my change and dollar bills in, never to take them out. As long as I was able to keep working, I didn't see any need to take out that money and buy things I didn't need.

When I got my license as a hairdresser, I washed and fixed people's hair for about fourteen years. But when Mama got sick with cancer, I went back to washing and ironing at home so I could take care of her.

Things changed after the war. I had been charging two dollars and fifty cents for a bundle of laundry, but as time passed people began to give me ten dollars a bundle. Some folks were switching to hand-cranked washing machines, but I kept using my cast-iron pot and the clothesline out back. I never needed much. My Bible got so tattered from use, I eventually taped it up to keep the pages in. I never needed a car; I always walked wherever I went, and that kept me healthy. I pushed a shopping cart back and forth to the grocery store about a mile down the road. I've got an old black-and-white TV. It gets one channel, but I rarely watched it. Instead, I read my Bible.

In '64, Mama died; in '67, my aunt passed on. And I've been by myself ever since. I've never thought of myself as alone though, because the Lord is always with me.

I kept right on working, even after the age most people retire. It was December of '94 when my hand started to swell. I was doing laundry for Lawyer McKenzie and his wife, and Mrs. McKenzie asked, "What's the matter with your hand?"

"Creeping arthritis," I said. "I've had a touch of it before, but it's really bothering me now." It was mighty distressing that I had to quit work at the age of 86. But I said, "Lord, I want You to stay by me and guide me and protect me in all things." And He sure did.

At the bank one day they asked me where I wanted my money to go when I passed on. Mr. Paul Laughlin—one of the officers there—sat down with me and spread out ten dimes on the desk. He told me that each dime represented 10 percent of my money. So I took a dime for the church and a dime for each cousin. That left six dimes to help with a dream I always had.

"I want to help some child go to college," I said. "I'm going to give the rest of my money to the University of Southern Mississippi, so deserving children can get a good education. I want to help African-American children who are eager for learning like I was, but whose families can't afford to send them to school."

Mr. Paul looked at me funny and said, "Miss Oseola, that means you'll be giving the school a hundred and fifty thousand dollars."

One hundred and fifty thousand dollars! I had never realized how much I had, and the amount about took my breath away! Lawyer McKenzie talked to me to make sure I still really wanted to follow through with my plan. Then we drew up the papers. He made sure I would still have enough money if I ever needed it, and the rest would be given out over the years ahead, year by year.

When the news of what I had done got out, folks from newspapers and magazines came around to find out who I was. I didn't see what the fuss was about, but invitations started arriving—to come visit the President in Washington, D.C., and the United Nations in New York City. I had never been outside of Mississippi, except to Niagara Falls one time long ago and the roar scared me so! But I went and received a Presidential Citizens Medal and was honored by the U.N. Who would have ever thought I would be making trips like that?

But of all the new people I met, the one who meant the most to me showed up right in my own front yard. That August a lovely young girl ran up and threw her arms around me. "Thank you, Miss McCarty," she said, "for helping me go to college."

It was a bright girl named Stephanie, who was about to begin her freshman year. She was the first to receive a one-thousand-dollar Oseola McCarty Scholarship. Stephanie had brought along her mother, a schoolteacher, her grandmother—a seamstress, and her twin brother, who was entering college also. We all sat visiting on the screened-in front porch. Right off, we felt like family.

Stephanie had wanted with all her heart to go to USM, but since her twin brother was starting his freshman year in college also, money was pretty tight. Although her grades were good and she had been president of the student body at Hattiesburg High, she kept missing out on scholarships. Nonetheless, she had gone ahead and applied to USM on faith, and her family had asked the Lord for help. Everyone in the Bullock family prayed for something to happen. Stephanie's mama kept telling her not to worry but to trust in the Lord that something good would come through.

"Lord, You've told us that if we asked, we would receive," Stephanie had prayed, *"so I'm asking for Your help."* Then she received a phone call telling her she would be the first person to receive an Oseola McCarty Scholarship. "Within minutes," Stephanie's mother told me, "the whole neighborhood knew!"

I'm so proud. I told Stephanie right away that I'm planning to be there for her graduation. Now I feel like I have a granddaughter.

I'm always surprised when people ask me, "Miss McCarty, why didn't you spend that money on yourself?" I just smile.

Thanks to the good Lord, I am spending it on myself. I'm investing in my dream.

WHITE SOCKS

JAN WILSON

For your Father knows what you need before you ask him.

MATTHEW 6:8 NIV

"THERE IS COMFORT IN THE FACT THAT GOD CAN NEVER BE TAKEN BY SURPRISE."

Ralph Waldo Emerson

Breakfast was finished just in time for us to peek at the sunrise over the Dominican coast and scramble onto the bus before it pulled away. Packed in among the medical team volunteers were large wooden boxes overflowing with medicine. Two large containers of drinking water were squeezed in alongside a sturdy green plastic tub filled with clothes. Some passengers carried smaller sacks of toiletries on their laps.

Each day this team traveled to another remote Dominican village to offer medical and spiritual care to the people. As we left the paved road behind, we saw barefoot men on horseback or working the fields with machetes. The roads were deeply rutted and washed out from the recent rains. When the bus finally arrived in front of the small school and one-room church, a lively crowd had already gathered.

Within forty-five minutes, a makeshift clinic was set up. Exam rooms, a pharmacy, and a health-education department were strategically placed to ensure a steady flow of traffic. Betty chose the cool, one-room church for the health-education team.

The people came to the health ed room to hear brief talks on hygiene and health maintenance as they waited for the medication to be dispensed. Some people had walked a long distance, missing both breakfast and lunch. As the morning coolness melted into the intense tropical heat of the afternoon, people stared with expressionless faces as heat or hunger overcame them. Though they were eager for information that could help them to improve their health, at times it was a challenge for us to hold their interest.

It was my "job" to award the prizes to the people. Betty gave me clues about what kind of prizes to choose. Small toiletry items, like soap or shampoo, were given to encourage discussion and to reward people's attempts to answer questions. If Betty saw someone who had no shoes or was more destitute than the others, she would look for an opportunity to bless them. As soon as they answered a question correctly, she would prompt me: "Give her something really nice."

Nice meant one of the larger items from the plastic treasure chest. Larger items included t-shirts, dresses, pants, or shoes. Early in the day it was fun to look at the variety of things to choose from and to try to match an item to the recipient. But by late afternoon, the chest was almost empty. Each time I heard Betty's cue, I would get a little more worried. Finally we had the last group of the day, and the large rewards were nearly gone, but there were still a few people yet to receive a prize.

Lord, please let us have something for each person, I prayed as I reached into the bin.

I could see the bottom. There were only a few small items left. This time when Betty said, "Give him something nice," the only prize left for a man was a pair of white socks. I was reluctant to give them out; they didn't seem like much of a prize. This man had seen me give shoes and pants and shirts to the others. Would he feel slighted that he was receiving only a pair of socks? I wanted to dig into my own bag for something larger, something nicer.

Then the still, small voice inside my heart urged, *Trust Me.*

I remembered the boy who gave his meager lunch to Jesus. Although it looked small compared to the need, he surrendered what he had available to feed others, and his gift was multiplied. I resisted the urge to apologize and say, "It's all we have left."

With a desire to grow in trust, I prayed, *Please let this small gift be a special blessing to him.* When I handed him the socks, his entire face beamed.

The medicine finally arrived with instructions attached. In a new flurry of activity, we called each person by name. As they came forward, we explained to each one how to take the medication and manage their illness. I called the name on the top of the sheet, quickly scanning the written instructions. This particular patient had athlete's foot, a common fungal infection. The instructions said to apply the antifungal cream daily and to keep the feet clean and dry. As a North American nurse, my next thought was to teach the patient about the importance of wearing clean, dry socks every day. However, since socks of any kind were beyond the reach of many of the people we had seen that day in the clinic, I planned to leave out that part of the instructions. Socks were a luxury that most people here just couldn't afford.

I hadn't noticed him approaching in the bustle of activity, but as he came closer, I recognized the same man who'd received the pair of clean white socks!! What I thought was a meager gift, was not only sufficient, it was perfect for him. Before I was even aware of his problem, God knew exactly what he needed.

As I handed him the medicine and gave the instructions, he smiled again, took the medication, and then he went on his way. I smiled in wonder that God used a pair of white socks that day to meet both his need and mine.

THE DAY I WALKED INTO GOD'S LOVE

NANCY L. ANDERSON

He heals the brokenhearted and binds up their wounds.

PSALM 147:3 NKJV

A scream pierced the darkness. It was a sound coming from my own throat, waking me from yet another nightmare. *Will they ever stop?* I asked myself, as the darkness of the night surrounded me.

I had endured too many years of undeserving abuse, and it had taken its toll on my mind and emotions. Even my subconscious was not immune to the fear and sadness those days brought into my life.

While dating my husband before we got married, he showed signs of being controlling and possessive. At the time I thought, *He must really care for me,* instead of thinking, *this*

"...WE MUST DEVELOP AND MAINTAIN THE CAPACITY TO FORGIVE. WHEN WE DISCOVER THIS, WE ARE LESS PRONE TO HATE OUR ENEMIES."

Dr. Martin Luther King, Jr.

might be a problem that could lead to severe consequences.

After we got married, our life together deteriorated at an alarming rate. What started out as verbal abuse soon escalated into physical abuse. Oh, there were days of love and fun, but the darkness of the hard days drowned out any happy memories.

"I'm sorry. It won't happen again. Don't leave me," he would plead, cruelly giving me hope for our future. That hope was short-lived as the episodes began again in a now familiar pattern. The day finally came when his words could no longer pacify my broken heart, spirit, and body. Instead they stung me as empty promises. Somehow I found the strength and courage to say, "No more!" And that chapter of my life closed.

The scars from that marriage left me to battle years of nightmares, resentment, and bitterness. I didn't know how to get past the emotional pain and anger I felt every time something reminded me of that place in my life. More than anything I wanted a sense of peace, but it escaped me.

Although we were no longer married, the anger lingered on and on—year after year—eating away at my heart. Someone would tell me, "You need to forgive," but I'd think, *How do you know what I've suffered? My anger is deserved.*

The body heals quickly, but my heart continued to hurt and my soul continued to weep. I wondered if healing would ever come. I searched for peace in churches, at conferences, in seminars, and by reading self-help books. Still, only bitterness and resentment came to me. I'd turn to God and cry out, *Help me, Lord! Where is Your peace?* He only spoke one word to my heart: *Forgive.*

I thought to myself, *But he's not even sorry! He doesn't want my forgiveness.* And then I'd find myself praying again, *Lord, it hurts to hate so much.*

As time went on, the memories didn't heal. I'd bury the anger. I'd hide the pain. But like a snake ready to attack, they would surface repeatedly, their venom poisoning my spirit. Years passed as my search for freedom from these controlling emotions went on.

As God continued to work on my heart, my attitude began to change. I began to pray, *Lord, I need Your forgiveness for hanging onto this anger. It keeps me far from You. I miss feeling Your closeness. Teach me to forgive.*

One day I noticed an advertisement for a special speaker who was coming to a nearby church. My heart pounded in my chest. Something prompted me to go there. As I listened to this speaker's message, God opened my heart to receive the answers I had sought for so long.

He spoke about the wonderful forgiveness God had already provided through His Son. Jesus Christ had sacrificed His life for me by dying on a cross. As the man shared, I began to gain a new understanding of God's love and His forgiveness.

I asked myself, *Was I so righteous and good that I didn't need forgiveness?* Only Christ lived a sinless life—He deserved to live. Yet He was willing to take my place on that dreadful cross!

I began to see forgiveness for what it truly was— undeserved pardon. The complete understanding of what Christ did for me led me to understand this concept. Yes, I had been hurt. And perhaps my abuser didn't deserve my pardon. But that is precisely why it is called forgiveness.

I sensed God's arms open wide, and I crawled into His embrace to be consoled and comforted. The Bible says, "He heals the brokenhearted and binds up their wounds" (Psalm 147:3 NKJV). That day He healed my broken heart. My anger and bitterness vanished as forgiveness broke forth. My disappointments faded as a new hope for the future began in my heart. Sadness dissolved and joy filled my life. Peace overtook me.

It all began the day I walked into God's love.

GIVEN TO GOD

LINDA HENSON

By wisdom a house is built, and through

understanding it is established.

PROVERBS 24:3 NIV

"FAMILY FACES
ARE LIKE
MAGIC
MIRRORS.
LOOKING AT
PEOPLE WHO
BELONG
TO US, WE
SEE THE PAST,
PRESENT, AND
FUTURE.
WE MAKE
DISCOVERIES
ABOUT
OURSELVES."
Gail Lumet Buckley

Is it possible for a newborn daughter to save the life of her mother? That's what happened in my case. All through the pregnancy Jim and I had problems. Everything started out so beautifully. Jim had a promising career as a minister, and I had always dreamed of becoming a pastor's wife. I thought we had the perfect marriage. After all, ministers taught others about faithfulness and purity. We were both young, attractive, and totally in love; people often commented that we were the perfect couple.

Everything was wonderful until Jim began to spend a lot of time with a new group of friends. It wasn't long afterward that it became common for Jim to stay out all night—rarely accounting for his evenings. Jim didn't even try to hide his activities. He actually had convinced himself that it was the "cool" thing to do. After all, his other close friends were doing it.

Then came the yearly "guy" thing. When he left for the annual meeting, I would feel sick inside. I could see his whole attitude deteriorate. Family life seemed less and less important to him. We began to argue a lot. Fear had overtaken me; fear of losing my home and our life together. I couldn't believe we had sunk to such depths. We believed the Bible, but it played less and less of a part in our lives. It had become just a source book, something Jim used as the basis for his weekly homily.

Our relationship was suffering. I could see I was losing my husband and I didn't handle any of it in a righteous way. I accused, criticized, cried, and totally aggravated the situation. We were both on a downhill spiral.

I began to toy with thoughts of ending the pain. Each time I opened the medicine cabinet I stared at the bottles of different types of pills and wondered which ones could be lethal in large doses.

In the midst of all the pain I found out I was pregnant. Through the months of my pregnancy, my swollen body didn't make me feel any better. My days seemed to grow darker and darker.

One morning the pains began, and only two hours later I was holding a bright shining light. In the midst of my darkness God had sent an angel to brighten my days. In my desperation I clung to that sweet baby girl—but it didn't seem to be enough. One day at a weak moment I put the baby in her crib and went to the closet where we kept a handgun high on the shelf. I tiptoed, stretched, and finally felt the cold, dark steel in my hand. I pulled it down and held it in both hands, thinking of the decision before me.

I heard a small cry from the crib, and I looked down into the face of my angel. I began to imagine what her life would be like growing up knowing that her mother had done such a thing. Somewhere deep inside I heard a voice saying, "I didn't create you for this." I fell to my knees and began to cry. I knew that God cared about my situation and had spoken to me. Sobs poured from the very depths of my heart. I felt I was at the bottom of a deep well, but as I looked up, I could see the light. Repentance poured from my soul to the ears of God. I lifted my baby from her bed and held her tightly.

It seemed I held on to her for days. One day at a time, I sought God's help to restore my life and mental attitude. I realized that I had to deal with my own attitudes and only God could change my husband. Little by little I felt inner healing taking place and to my surprise, the more I released my husband's problems to God, the more I saw change take place in him. We were becoming a close-knit family again.

Just as we were experiencing the hand of God on our lives, a small church on the other side of the state requested that we come. I knew it was divine leading. We were finally ready to be the spiritual leaders we had been "called" to be. My daughter was still a source of inspiration to me, but I knew that perhaps I clung to her more than I should.

When she was five years old she caught a cold that didn't seem to go away. On Christmas Eve she was terribly ill. Finally, I couldn't stand it any longer and insisted we rush her to the emergency room. She had a high fever and as I held her in the car, I was terrified that we would lose her. All the way to the hospital I prayed. I wept and clung tightly to the small form in the blanket. As we pulled into the hospital, I whispered, "God, she's Yours. I give her to You. Please take care of her."

The doctors swept her from my arms. Nurses ushered us into the waiting room. Waiting rooms scream with pain— wives wondering if their husbands will survive heart attacks, children wondering if their mothers will return home; pain is everywhere.

It seemed like an eternity before anyone returned to speak

to us. A nurse came to relate the doctor's message: "It's possible that she has spinal meningitis." The words sent a chill through me. I called my mother who knows how to pray. Others from our church were praying too. All night we prayed, sometimes in the chapel, sometimes at her bedside.

In the wee hours of the morning the nurse came into our room and told us that she was out of danger; she only had pneumonia—and they could treat pneumonia. At that moment, I began to rejoice and thank God.

Through the years my daughter and I have shared a very special bond. What a delight she has been to me.

Now grown, my daughter travels abroad in diplomatic service and I know that she is in situations of potential danger much of the time. But long ago, and with great trust, I placed her in the hands of an ever faithful God. She belongs to Him, though I believe with all of my heart she was put into my life as a special gift from the Father.

SIMPLY LET GO

KAREN O'CONNOR

"For I know the plans I have for you," says the LORD, "plans to prosper you and not to harm you, plans to give you hope and a future."

JEREMIAH 29:11-12 NIV

"IT IS BETTER TO FORGIVE TOO MUCH THAN TO CONDEMN TOO MUCH."

Anonymous

I thought about her. I dreamed about her. I saw her in every woman I met. Some even had her name, Cathy. Others had her deep-set blue eyes or curly dark hair. Even the slightest resemblance turned my stomach into a knot.

Weeks, months, years passed. Was I never to be free of this woman who had pursued my husband, Jack, and then, following our divorce, married him? My resentment, guilt, and anger drained the life out of everything I did. I went into counseling, attended self-help classes, and enrolled in seminars and workshops. I read books and talked to anyone who would listen.

I ran. I walked the beach. I drove for miles to nowhere. I screamed into my pillow at night, prayed and blamed myself. I did everything I knew how to do—except surrender. *How could this have happened?* I asked myself over and over.

I had been happy before she came into my life—at least I thought I was. My days were simple, predictable, and filled with good things—the stuff most women long for: a successful husband, children I loved, tennis with my friends three mornings a week, church on Sundays, summer vacations, a lovely home, and a beautiful car. What more could I have wanted?

Suddenly everything changed. My life would never be the same again. I didn't like what I saw in myself. I hated the man I had loved for over twenty years—my husband, the father of my children. I hated the other woman. And I began to hate myself. *How can any good come from such pain and grief?* I repeatedly asked.

I did not receive an answer right away. But I know now that God did have a response—which He gave to me one Saturday. I attended a day-long seminar held at a church in my neighborhood. It focused on the healing power of forgiveness. After the introduction, some discussion and sharing, the leader invited participants to close their eyes and picture someone in their lives they had not forgiven—for whatever reason—real or imagined. Cathy's name loomed large in my mind.

Next, he asked whether or not we'd be willing to forgive that person. My stomach churned again. My hands were suddenly wet, and my head throbbed. I felt I had to get out of that room, but something kept me in my seat.

How could I forgive a person like Cathy? She not only hurt me—she hurt my children as well. I decided to turn my attention to other people in my life. My mother—she is easy to forgive. Or my friend Ann, or even my former high-school English teacher. I could forgive anyone but Cathy. But there was no escape. Her name persisted, and the image of her face on my mind would not fade.

Then a voice within gently asked, *Are you ready to let go of this? To release her? To forgive yourself as well?* It wasn't an audible voice—but rather an impression, and I knew it was the Holy Spirit pursuing me.

I turned hot, then cold. I began to shake. I was certain everyone around me could hear my heart beating. Yes, I was willing. I couldn't hold on to my anger any longer. It was killing me. In that moment, without doing anything else, an incredible shift occurred within me—I simply let go!

Suddenly I was willing to do something I had doggedly resisted for years. For the first time since my husband had left, I gave control of my life to the Holy Spirit. I released my grip on Cathy, on Jack, and on myself. I let go of my rage and resentment—just like that.

As I sat there, energy rushed through every cell of my body. My mind became alert and my heart lightened. Unexpectedly I realized that as long as I have separated myself from even one person, I have separated myself from God.

How self-righteous I had been. How judgmental. How important it had been for me to be right, no matter what the cost. And it had cost me plenty—my health, my spontaneity, my vitality, and most importantly, my relationship with God.

I had no idea what would occur next, but it didn't matter. That night I slept straight into the morning. I had no dreams, no haunting face, and no reminders.

If it had been up to me alone, I don't know if I would have had the courage or the generosity to make the first move. But it was not up to me. There was no way to mistake the power of the Holy Spirit within me.

The following Monday I walked into my office and wrote Cathy a letter. The words spilled onto the page without effort.

"Dear Cathy," I began. "On Saturday morning...," and I proceeded to tell her what had occurred during the seminar. I also told her how I had hated her for what she had done to my marriage and to my family, and, as a result, how I had denied both of us the healing power of forgiveness. I apologized for my hateful thoughts. I signed my name, slipped the letter into an envelope, and popped it in the mailbox—without looking back.

On Wednesday afternoon of the same week, the phone rang.

"Karen?"

I recognized her voice.

"It's Cathy," she said softly.

I was surprised that my stomach remained calm. My hands were dry, and my voice remained steady and sure. I listened more than I talked—which was unusual for me. I found myself actually interested in what Cathy had to say.

She thanked me for the letter, and she acknowledged my courage in writing it. Then she told me how sorry she was— for everything. She talked briefly about her regret, her sadness for me, for my children, and more. Everything I had longed to hear from her, she said that day.

As I replaced the receiver, however, another insight came to me. I realized that as nice as it was to hear her words of apology, they didn't really matter. They paled in comparison to what God was teaching me. Buried deep in the trauma of my divorce, I found the truth I had searched for all my life without even knowing it. God is my Source, my Strength, my very Supply. He alone can bring about lasting healing.

For four years I had been caught in the externals, the reasons, the lies, the excuses, the jealousy, and the anger. But now I had a clear experience of what, until then, had been a stack of psychological insights. I suddenly understood that no one can truly hurt me as long as I remain in God's hands. No one can rob me of my joy—unless I allow them to. My life is mine, and every experience, no matter how painful or confusing, can serve my spiritual growth. Every moment has its purpose if I am serving the Lord.

Since then I have started over again in another city—free of the binding ties of jealousy, anger, and resentment—free to experience all that God has for me. My children are healing, and our home is filled with peace and laughter. Yes, I thought I was happy when I lived that shallow, predictable life, but now I know true happiness—walking one step at a time behind the Great Shepherd who leads me on the paths He has chosen.

MILEY

KAREN MAJORIS-GARRISON

Freely you have received, freely give.

MATTHEW 10:8 NKJV

"EXTENDING YOUR HAND IS EXTENDING YOURSELF."

Rod McKuen

I was in the prima donna, self-centered age of seventeen, and my motives were simple—to enhance my final grade in Health Assistant class. To accomplish this goal, I decided to volunteer at the nearby convalescent center.

For weeks I grumbled to my boyfriend. "I can't believe I'm stuck taking care of old people for free!" He agreed. The bright yellow uniforms my classmates and I were required to wear made matters even worse. On our first day at the center, the nurses took one look at our sunshiny apparel and nicknamed us "The Yellow Birds."

During my scheduled days, I complained to the other "yellow birds" how emptying bedpans, changing soiled linens, and spoon-feeding pureed foods to mumbling mouths were not jobs any teenager should have to do.

A tedious month passed, and then I met Lily. I was given a tray of food and told to take it to her room. Her bright blue eyes appraised me as I entered, and I soon became aware of the kindness that rested behind them. After talking with her for a few minutes, I realized why I hadn't noticed Lily before, although I had been past her room numerous times. Lily, unlike so many of the other residents, was soft-spoken and undemanding. My first day at the convalescent home, I discovered the staff had their favorite patients—usually those with character that stood out in some way. From joke-tellers to singers, the louder and more rambunctious the patient, the more attention they received.

Something inside of me immediately liked Lily, and strangely, I even began to enjoy our talks during my visits to her room. It didn't take long for me to realize that Lily's genuine kindness stemmed from her relationship with God.

"Come here," she said and smiled to me one rainy afternoon. "Sit down. I have something to show you." She lifted a small photo album and began to turn the pages. "This was my Albert. See him there? Such a handsome man." Her voice softened even more as she pointed to a pretty little girl sitting on top of a fence. "And that was our darling Emmy when she was eight years old."

A drop of wetness splattered on the plastic cover and I quickly turned to Lily. Her eyes were filled with tears. "What is it?" I whispered, covering her hand with my own.

She didn't answer right away, but as she turned the pages I noticed that Emmy was not in any other photographs. "She died from cancer that year," Lily told me. "She'd been in and out of hospitals most of her life, but that year she went home to Jesus."

"I'm so sorry," I said.

"It's okay," she smiled slightly, meeting my eyes. "God is good to those who love Him, and He has a plan for every life, Karen. We need to open our hearts to Him whether we understand His ways or not. Only then can we find true peace." She turned to the last page. Inside the worn album was one more picture of a middle-aged Lily standing on tiptoes and kissing a clown's cheek.

"That's my Albert," she laughed, recalling happier memories. "After Emmy died, we decided to do something to help the children at the hospitals. We'd been so disturbed by the dismal surroundings while Emmy was hospitalized." Lily went on to explain how Albert decided to become "Smiley the Clown."

"Emmy was always smiling, even in the worst of times. So

I scraped together what fabric I could find and sewed this costume for Albert." She clasped her hands in joy. "The children loved it! Every weekend, we volunteered at the hospitals to bring smiles and gifts to the children."

"But you were so poor! How did you manage that?" I asked in amazement.

"Well," she grinned, "smiles are free, and the gifts weren't anything fancy." She closed the album and leaned back against her pillows. "Sometimes the local bakers donated goodies, or when we were really hurting for money, we'd take a litter of pups from our farm. The children loved petting them. After Albert died, I noticed how faded and worn the costume was, so I rented one and dressed as Smiley myself; that is...until my first heart attack, about ten years ago."

When I left Lily's room that day, I couldn't think of anything other than how generous she and Albert had been to children who weren't even their own.

Graduation day neared, and on my last day of volunteer services at the ward, I hurried to Lily's room. She was asleep, curled into a fetal position from stomach discomfort. I stroked her brow, worrying about who would care for her the way I did. She didn't have any family, and most of the staff neglected her except for her basic needs, which were met with polite abruptness. At times, I wanted to proclaim Lily's virtues to the

staff, but she'd stop me, reminding me that the good things
she'd done in life were done without thoughts of self.
"Besides," she would say, "doesn't the good Lord tell us to
store our treasures in heaven and not on this earth?"

Lily must have sensed my inner torment above her bed that
day as she opened her eyes and touched my hand. "What is it,
dear?" she asked, her voice concerned and laced with pain.

"I'll be back in two weeks," I told her, explaining about my
high-school graduation. "And then I'll visit you every day. I
promise."

She sighed and squeezed my fingers. "I can't wait for you
to tell me all about it."

Two weeks later, I rushed back to the center, bubbling with
excitement and anxious to share with Lily the news of my
graduation events. With a bouquet of lilies in my hand, I
stepped into her clean, neat, but unoccupied room. The bed was
made and as I searched for an answer to Lily's whereabouts,
my heart already knew the answer.

I threw the flowers on the bed and wept.

A nurse gently touched my shoulder. "Were you one of the
yellow birds?" she asked. "Is your name Karen?" I nodded and
she handed me a gift-wrapped box. "Lily wanted you to have
this. We've had it since she died because we didn't know how
to get in touch with you."

It was her photo album. Written on the inside cover was the scripture Jeremiah 29:11 NIV: "For I know the plans I have for you," declares the Lord, "plans to prosper you and not to harm you, plans to give you hope and a future." I clutched it to my chest and departed.

Three weeks later, my horrified boyfriend stood before me. "You can't be serious!" he said, pacing back and forth. "You look ridiculous."

We were in my bedroom and as I tried to view myself in the mirror, he blocked my reflection. "You can't be serious," he repeated. "How in the world did you pay for that thing anyway?"

"With my graduation money," I answered.

"Your what?" he exclaimed, shaking his head. "You spent the money that we saved for New York on that?"

"Yep," I replied, stringing on my rubber nose. "Life should be more about giving than receiving."

"This is just great," he muttered, helping me tie the back of the costume. "And what am I supposed to tell someone when they ask me my girlfriend's name? That it's Bozo?"

I looked at my watch. I needed to hurry if I wanted to make it on time to the children's hospital.

"Nope," I answered, kissing him quickly on the cheek. "Tell them it's Smiley...Smiley the Clown."

$\mathcal{R}$UNNING IN THE RAIN

LAURA L. SMITH

Run with patience the particular race that God has set before us.

HEBREWS 12:1 TLB

"PERSEVERANCE
IS NOT A
LONG RACE;
IT IS MANY
SHORT RACES,
ONE AFTER
THE OTHER."
Walter Elliott

SLOP, SLOP, pitter, patter, SLOP, SLOP, pitter, patter. My running shoes rhythmically pound the asphalt of our neighborhood as the melodious rain joins to create a symphony of splashing.

It is forty-two degrees.

My husband came home from work early and built a roaring blaze in the fireplace. Our children are dancing in circles, celebrating its warmth while I am outside running.

I wanted to be inside with my hands wrapped around a cup of rich, sweet, steaming cocoa, nestled beside Michael reading Dr. Seuss's silly rhymes, and watching Mackenzie cautiously biting the charred edges of a roasted marshmallow, anticipating its gooey center.

I didn't want to go out, but my body needed to stretch and flex, and my mind needed to recharge.

Sometimes I am too content in what I am doing to be motivated to go to church, or to read my Bible, or to pray. And yet, my spirit craves these things. When I allow time to tune the instrument that is my soul, I always feel refreshed and rejuvenated.

Running mirrors my faith walk.

The heavy perfume in the damp air signals to my nose that the yard of "The Flower Man" is just around the bend. All seasons of the year are as constant as God's love. The land that spans from Mr. Stein's front door to the street is triumphantly adorned with vibrant purples, yellows, and oranges. Drops of rain sparkle on the beautiful blooms forming iridescent pools on the silky petals.

A minivan splashes through a puddle, crashing through the water-like cymbals, and sprays my already soaked body. I wave at the family and think, *What do they think of me, running in this miserable weather? Do they think I'm a lunatic? Or am I an inspiration? I hope they see me exercising and vow to do something healthy for their own bodies.*

Some days no one sees me at all. My footsteps drum up and down the vacant streets, tapping out my personal rhythm. I am alone with no one else to motivate me, but I am never lonely.

Isn't it the same with my faith? I attend church publicly and let friends know about my beliefs. I hope my actions serve as a catalyst for good in others' lives. Yet, in the privacy of my room, no one sees me on my knees praying to God for forgiveness, peace, and salvation. I am called to spread His Word, but I also treasure my personal relationship with my Lord.

I cough the rancid taste of exhaust out of my lungs.

As the family in the van speeds away, I picture Brian, Mackenzie, and Michael frolicking around the fireplace. I miss them when I run alone, but it wouldn't be fair to drag my four-year-old, my one-year-old, or even my husband out in this downpour.

On seventy-five-degree, sunny spring days, I do sometimes bring them with me. Brian pushes the doublewide jog stroller. I point out squirrels, airplanes, or clouds to the kids, and we all sing with the sparrows. Those runs remind me of our family when we sing hymns or pray together. We are one family, four people, bonded together in love and united with God, the Creator of the universe.

On the left is Dr. McCue's ash-gray A-frame house. He is inside today, staying dry, but most days he is out watering the grass, painting shutters, or pruning trees. The retired dean of the university offers sage words to passers-by. Too rushed to listen to his lengthy, albeit kind stories, I often keep running and give only a quick wave. But when I take the time to stop, I am rewarded with tales spun and lessons peppered with insight and experience. Like our Lord, he shares his wisdom freely to those who stop long enough to listen.

Rain trickles down the sides of my red baseball cap blurring my view. Unlike runs when my legs fly across the pavement, today I feel as if I am wading through Jell-O. With my faith I have "on" days where I am the Christian I profess to be, and I have "off" days where I struggle to serve God.

WOOOOOOF! WOOF!

At the sound of Floyd's ferocious barking something inside me snaps like a broken string on a harp. Floyd is a Doberman pincher who lives at the end of Arbor Trail, the final loop of my route. Why am I so frightened by the cacophony of his barking although I know where Floyd lives and what he will do? I could yell back and shake my finger like a fool; or believing I'm not vulnerable, I could enter his yard in hopes of bullying him. I choose to ignore the dog.

Like Satan, Floyd tempts me and frightens me. But both the Doberman and the devil are contained—one by a physical fence and the other by my electric fence of faith. Neither the devil nor the dog can hurt me when I turn away from them and toward God. It is only when I choose to take matters into my own hands, to cross over the boundary line onto their turf, that

I am in danger.

I turn wide, staying on the left-hand side of the road. Isn't that peculiar? Going against the rest of the world and facing traffic keeps me safe. God asks me to do the same thing, so I won't fall in line with the traffic patterns of the world. He wants me to resist temptation and face worldly things head-on. When I am set apart from larger vehicles crossing my path, I can see oncoming obstacles and protect myself from the peril they might bring.

Lightning streaks through the sky. My heart thumps like a mallet picking notes on a xylophone. The rain has evolved into a thunderstorm as I face the crescendo, the steepest hill on my path.

But I know I can make it. Just beyond the hill is my home. I don't have much farther to go.

I know I can do it.

I am a runner.

And I am a Christian.

THE MIRROR

LINDA HENSON

If we are living in the light of God's presence, just as Christ does,
then we have wonderful fellowship and joy with each other.

1 JOHN 1:7 TLB

"NOTHING IS SO SOOTHING TO OUR SELF-ESTEEM AS TO FIND OUR BAD TRAITS IN OUR FOREBEARS. IT SEEMS TO ABSOLVE US."
Van Wyck Brooks

I trembled a bit as I slowly slipped my finger under the seal of the envelope. Both of my daughters are strong, productive young women who reluctantly agreed to my proposal. I had just finished my first year of graduate studies in counseling. The first year is the hardest; each student is required to receive ten hours of personal counseling. I didn't think I had anything that needed "fixing;" on the outside we were a happy, balanced family. I had discovered you can't help others if you can't look at yourself. As the layers ripped off through those sessions, I began to feel exposed. Maybe I wasn't as "Okay" as I had thought.

I did the scariest thing I could imagine. I called each of my daughters and asked them to write me a letter telling me what they felt about my parenting. I asked them for a "no-holds-barred" response. The weeks of waiting for their replies were horrendous for me. My mind went through every experience I could remember, wondering if the girls would say I was unfair, or too hard on them. It was an open invitation for them to let me have it. Painful as it might be, I truly wanted to know. I wondered, *Could I learn from the past?*

I was the disciplinarian in our family. My husband is an easy-going phlegmatic who likes to be the good guy. I was raised with rules and regulations and had learned that there was a price to pay when rules were broken. My siblings and I all seemed to be responsible adults so I assumed that the parenting model I experienced was the best one to follow.

My counseling sessions had proven to be heart-wrenching. It was necessary to look at the effect of our parents' input into our lives. I've always struggled with this part of counseling; I need to take responsibility for the choices I've made and refuse to blame my parents.

It was important to realize our past shapes the way we handle life, so I was forced to hold up a mirror to my life and willingly see the negative aspects of the model my parents set before me.

My mother was very controlling; everyone knew she spoke for the family. My dad went along with whatever she wanted just to survive. I began to let the memories come back. I felt the fear of my mother's wrath. Did I receive beatings? No, but the fear was there. Even the look of disapproval, disappointment, or the tone of voice from a parent can go deep into a child's heart and I realized my heart had been pierced.

One Saturday when I was a teen, a group of teenagers from our local church planned a day at the State Park. It was too cool to swim so we knew we'd have to look for other activities such as hiking or boating. My mother had never learned to swim, and she was determined that we wouldn't go near the water if she wasn't around. I happened to mention that I needed money to help pay for the rental of a rowboat.

"You are not to go out in a boat!" was her order.

"But, Mom, that's what everybody will do."

"You heard me."

I was right. Everyone in the group rented boats and spent the day on the water. I sat alone on the beach all afternoon. Why didn't I just go ahead and go with the rest of the group? Somehow, the fear of Mom finding out was so strong that a miserable afternoon seemed easier to take. There was a mental control that followed me through much of my life. I hadn't realized it until the counselor held up the "mirror."

During my engagement to my husband we would return home after a date and sit in the driveway for a few minutes before going inside with the family. Of course, we weren't going to go "too far" with my parents right inside; but invariably, my mother would begin to flash the porch light on and off signaling that we were to come in immediately. Not all of the fear was bad. It kept me from making mistakes that could have had negative impacts on my life. There is a measure of parental fear that is healthy. However, the line is very easy to cross and after experiencing the counseling, I feared that I could have easily stepped over it with my own children without realizing it. Only they could decide, and I was about to read their assessments.

Had I imparted that same controlling fear to my daughters? Did they see me as I saw my mother? Children see our imperfections and learn to live with them. Did my daughters have to find mechanisms to deal with the kind of parent I had been? All of these questions ran through my mind as I tore away the envelope that held my older daughter's response.

Tears flowed down my cheeks as kindness flowed through her words. I had asked for harsh truth and yet I received beautiful compliments. Most of the letter reminisced the good moments we had enjoyed. At the end, though, was this thought: *Mom, I wish you had talked to me more.*

I was startled. We had talked. But I realized her desire. I was never open to sharing my thoughts, pain, or longings with her. I understood that she didn't know who I really was. She knew me as one who fed, clothed, and provided emotional support, but in my desire to be the picture of a good mother, I had withheld the real me.

The second letter stared at me. Our older daughter had always been an easy-to-please child who gave little or no resistance to our directions, but the second? She was another story. It seemed she always pushed the line. She had an outlook on life that said, "I think I can fly!" Now, I was about to read her opinions on my parenting skills. I braced myself. We had butted heads repeatedly through her teen years. But, to my amazement, her letter began as the first, with sharing the things she appreciated. Tears would not describe my response. Opened floodgates might be a better reflection of the scene.

When I read the second part of her letter, I nearly dropped the page. I decided the girls had collaborated, for I read nearly the same phrase: *"Mom, I wish you had shared who you are with me."*

I ran to the phone and called each one of them asking if they had talked and agreed upon their responses; but each assured me they had not spoken about what went into their letters. Actually, they had been as nervous about writing them as I had been about reading them.

Following my telephone conversations with the girls, I had

to go to God. I had hidden behind walls that now were revealed. Could I trust that He would heal the hurts and ease the pain as I bared my inner self?

In the days since, I've made a conscious effort to take special times with each of my daughters to sit and talk with them openly. I've shared times of my life that were full of pain. I've shared embarrassing moments. I hadn't realized that withholding some of the unlovely things of my life had presented a level of perfection to them that they felt they could never attain. It is a relief to find that sharing my imperfections has drawn us closer together. With a lot of hard work and dedication, the love of two amazing daughters, and the tender grace of a merciful God, we have all been set free to love each other completely—without reservation.

HER WORK ISN'T FINISHED YET!

JOAN CLAYTON

"TODAY A NEW
SUN RISES
FOR ME;
EVERYTHING
LIVES,
EVERYTHING
IS ANIMATED,
EVERYTHING
SEEMS TO
SPEAK TO ME
OF MY
PASSION,
EVERYTHING
INVITES ME TO
CHERISH IT."
Anne de Lenclos

"For I know the plans I have for you," declares the LORD,
"plans to prosper you and not to harm you,
plans to give you hope and a future."

JEREMIAH 29:11 NIV

Around in the spiral I swirled. A dark tunnel grasped me. My head ached with dizziness! At the end of the tunnel I saw two angels standing by my bed, dressed in white robes and hoods.

"We have to send her back. Her work isn't finished yet!"

The other angel impatiently replied, "Well, hurry up, because she's about to die!"

I quickly awakened to the sickening smell of ether. At sixteen, I was a senior in high school and plagued with recurring ear infections. The doctor had hoped that the removal of my adenoids would end the siege of illnesses I continually experienced.

The implications while I was under the anesthesia left me in a daze. *I dare not tell a soul or they'll think I'm crazy!* But I thought of the experience often and hoped that someday I might understand the mystery.

"Her work isn't finished yet," the angel in my dream had said. I wondered many times what my work was—my purpose.

The surgery was a success. Years later I graduated from college, married my "knight in shining armor." I had the most wonderful husband in the world, a lovely, brand-new home, and two beautiful little boys. I thought I had everything, but the storybook pages of my life suddenly shattered under a cloud of darkness. Depression struck—when Mark was three, and Lance only eighteen months old—my world seemed to fall apart.

I awoke one night, stricken with panic. Deep despair engulfed me. The weight of thick, cold depression strained my breathing. It seemed to smother and stifle the entire room. Questions came: *Who am I, and why am I here? What is my purpose in life?*

I looked at my husband, Emmitt, lying asleep beside me. I can't tell him how I feel. I'll have to hide it from him. Tormenting thoughts came so fast and furious that I wanted to cry out. The pain was unbearable. *Will this night ever end?* I wondered. *If it does, then what?*

My thinking process was completely disrupted. *What is happening to me?* I wanted to run somewhere and never stop, screaming all the way. Pain and confusion gripped me in their frightening fingers, and I felt I couldn't get away!

I felt like a zombie in the days and weeks that followed. I continually thought, *I am useless, good for nothing, a ship without a sail.*

I saw the anxiety and concern on Emmitt's face as he left for his teaching job each morning. I felt sorry for him, but I remained completely helpless to do anything. He took me to our family doctor many times.

One day the doctor said: "There is nothing I can find wrong with you physically, so I am going to send you to the best source I know to deal with emotional illness."

He's sending me to a shrink! I remember thinking. *Everyone thinks I've lost it!*

Emmitt, a teacher starting out with a low salary, went to the bank. Thank God for a compassionate banker. He loaned us the money that it would take for expert care. Emmitt left our precious boys with my mother, and together we began the long journey toward my recovery.

The ride to the hospital still remains a blur in my mind. I clung to Emmitt. The doctor said I needed to be hospitalized for thirty days—telling Emmit it would be best if he left immediately. We held each other as I sobbed uncontrollably.

"Don't leave me! I can't live without you!" I cried as Emmitt tried to leave. He desperately tried to remove my arms from him, as he cried himself. But we both knew it had to be. I simply could not function anymore as a wife or as a mother. Surely there must be a greater purpose for my life. But the darkness had blotted out all possibility of rational thought.

I discovered later that Emmitt almost turned back toward the hospital several times while driving home. I thought of *Mark and Lance without a mommy at home* and with that thought, I cried myself to sleep many nights.

The woman in the next room had been in a car wreck and screamed continually. Walking over to look out the window of my hospital's second-story room, I thought about jumping, and at the end of my rope, I prayed:

Lord, I can do nothing without You. I am nothing without You. I'm so alone. I'm so scared. My poor little boys need a mother. Emmitt needs a wife. The bills are mounting up. I feel like I'm going down for the last time. So here I am, Lord. I give my life to You. I give myself completely to You. Whatever You choose to do with me is all right. I love You, Jesus.

Immediately, a peace came over me that even to this day I cannot explain. I was flooded with peace, perfect peace. I realized that my life no longer belonged to me. I was in my Father's hands, and He had a purpose for me. My prayer became the turning point. And at the point of complete surrender, I put it all in God's hands.

In the course of a month, I received eight treatments. Each treatment wiped me out for twenty-four hours. The horrific headaches kept me bedridden. I couldn't eat. I slept an entire day and night after each episode. But the rest became a time of healing for me.

During the third week of my stay, I began to make friends throughout the hospital. One patient especially took me under her wing. An older lady, hospitalized with diabetes, became my cheerleader. "Honey," she would say, "things will be all right. You will find joy again because God is with you, and He never abandons His own!"

On the twenty-eighth morning of my stay, I asked the doctor, "What am I doing here? I have a loving husband and two precious boys at home who need me!"

My doctor had heard the words he longed to hear. "Now, you are ready to go home."

I hugged my doctor good-bye. I told each friend in the hospital how thankful I was for their friendship. Their support and love had helped my recovery.

As I prepared to leave, I washed my hair and set it in

rollers. I wanted to shave my legs because after twenty-eight days they looked gross! Most of all, I wanted to be beautiful when Emmitt walked in that afternoon. I looked at the clock. *Eight o'clock* I thought, *I still have plenty of time.*

At that moment I heard familiar footsteps coming down the hall. I looked up to see the most handsome man I had ever laid eyes on. Emmitt swooped me up and held me tight—rollers, hairy legs, and all. "You're so beautiful," he said. The happiest day of my life had come, and God had answered my prayers for deliverance.

We arrived home to see two happy little boys, whom I could not have loved more. I walked out of the hospital cold turkey. No drugs. No tranquilizers. Emmitt talked to me all night long, telling me of his love. I had to laugh when he said: "You know what? Everyone has some kind of problem, and we all act strange sometimes."

Emmitt's prayers for me each night gave me peace, as he committed our lives to God. And five years later, a new, precious little boy, a little angel we called "Lane," blessed our happy home.

If you break a leg it's honorable, but emotional illness seems to have a stigma attached to it. Now I know who I am in Jesus! I now tell my story because there is a Great Physician who longs to heal all of us—even those suffering from depression—and He has a purpose for every life.

Someone walked up to me the other day at a book signing. "Are you somebody?" she asked.

"I certainly am." I replied. "I'm a writer."

My emotional illness took place many years ago. I've since retired after thirty-one years of teaching in the public schools—a job I loved.

In my retirement, I have written seven books and published around 450 articles. I am the religion columnist for our local newspaper. I have been nominated three times in "Who's Who Among American Teachers" and have been published so far in two different "Chicken Soup" books.

Early in my life I had heard the words of an angel in a dream, "Her work isn't finished yet." I will continue to write.

I will continue to share Jesus' love. I have finally found my purpose.

A KNOCK ON
THE DOOR

NANCY B. GIBBS

Behold, I stand at the door, and knock: if any man hear

my voice, and open the door, I will come in to him,

and will sup with him, and he with me.

R E V E L A T I O N   3 : 2 0

"IF A
WINDOW OF
OPPORTUNITY
APPEARS,
DON'T PULL
DOWN
THE SHADE."

Tom Peters

We all know the feeling. It had been a busy workweek and
Saturday morning finally arrived. I slept a little later than usual
and decided to relax the morning away. As I climbed out of the
bed, I glanced at the mirror, by accident of course, and saw
more than I bargained for. A bad hair day wouldn't come close
to a description of what I saw.

Determined not to let it ruin the day, I slipped on my robe,
tried to forget the image I had just seen, and picked up the
newspaper. When I walked into my living room, I saw blankets

and pillows spread out on the couch. My precious poodle, Daisey, had strewn toys across the floor, alongside Sunshine's catnip balls.

Who cares? I thought, as I flopped down on the couch to relax. But just about the time I got comfortable, I heard a knock on the door.

"Oh, no," I groaned. "It's too early for company." I rushed to the bathroom, tried to tame my hair, and quickly washed my face. I hurriedly threw on some clothes, ran back into the living room and gathered up the blankets and pillows, then kicked the pet toys into the corner of the room. I threw the linens in the bedroom, and after taking a deep breath, finally opened the door.

No one was there. For the rest of the day, I wondered who it was that had knocked on my door. I had only heard one knock. Perhaps I was so busy trying to clean up that I failed to hear the second.

One day, quite a few years earlier, I had heard another knock. That time it wasn't a knock on the door to my house, but a knock on the door to my heart. As I sat quietly, I tried to pretend that I didn't hear it. But there was no doubt as I sat a few pews back in that large church that Jesus was calling me to open the door of my heart to Him.

On that pew my heart began to pound, while my hands

began to tremble. I had never felt emotion like I felt that day. Since I hadn't regularly attended church, I didn't know what to make of what I was experiencing. But I knew that something was happening to me that I could not explain with words. I began to talk to myself in response to the persistent knocking.

"I have too much to straighten up in my life right now. When I get it all worked out, then I'll open the door. Please understand that I can't let You in my heart while I have sin in my life," I whispered, during the first verse of the invitation hymn.

When the verse ended, I let out a sigh of relief, but immediately the choir began singing the second verse. The pastor asked everyone to bow in prayer. I was glad to put down the hymnal and close my eyes. Maybe no one would see how badly I was shaking. It seemed as if that particular verse lasted forever. Again, I heard a knock. This time it was even louder than the first.

"Next week," I whispered as the second verse ended. Again I sighed as the choir became quiet. But the music didn't stop. I looked up, and the pastor was standing directly in front of me. At that moment, I couldn't contain myself any longer. I opened the door to my heart. As tears streamed down my face, I didn't walk to the altar—I ran. Jesus met me there, despite the sin in my heart. He was there to help me clean it up, and more than twenty-five years later, He continues to help me handle any chaos in my life.

The person who knocked on the door to my house that Saturday wasn't nearly as patient as Jesus had been when He knocked on the door to my heart. He made sure that I heard Him, and He gave me an ample amount of time to answer. Thankfully, He wasn't concerned about the clutter in my heart, because that day He accepted me just as I was.

That Sunday morning marked a brand-new beginning in my life. I've grown closer to God as I have diligently studied His Word and sought Him out in prayer. And while I may continue to have difficulties with a cluttered house and strewn pet toys at times—my heart is a place of peace and welcome for the Visitor who profoundly changed my life.

I LEARNED THE TRUTH AT SEVENTEEN

TONYA RUIZ

For the Lord does not see as man sees; for man looks at the outward appearance, but the LORD looks at the heart.

1 SAMUEL 16:7 NKJV

"THE KIND OF BEAUTY I WANT MOST IS THE HARD-TO-GET KIND THAT COMES FROM WITHIN— STRENGTH, COURAGE, DIGNITY.

Ruby Dee

"I learned the truth at seventeen, that love was meant for beauty queens...." Those words spilled from our car radio in 1975, and I believed them. As a scrawny twelve-year-old, I believed that if I were beautiful, my life would be perfect.

Four years later at age sixteen, I was chosen from more than 200 girls to go to Paris and become a fashion model. My agent told me, "Your rail-thin body, shiny blonde hair, and sky blue eyes will be your passport to success!" *Teen* magazine wrote an article about my life called, "A Model's Success Story: It's like something that happens in the movies!"

My "glamorous" and "exciting" life was filled with dancing, drinking, dating, and parties. Life was a thrill a minute. It never occurred to me that my excessive eating and drinking could affect how I looked, but it did. At the modeling agency one day, I was told, "You look puffy and tired!"

At a photo shoot the hairstylist painstakingly arranged my hair in an elegant upsweep. I put on a gown that was waiting for me. The assistants set the lighting, and I settled into position. Then the photographer scrutinized me up and down, and said, "No. No good. You can go home." My first taste of rejection as a model was devastating—I felt as if I had been punched in the stomach. On the way home, I purchased a huge chocolate bar and overindulged.

Six months later, I was living on my own, in an apartment in New York. One evening my mom called. "Your agent, Valerie, called us and said you've gained a lot of weight. She said you're fat. Tonya, are you fat?"

"Yes!" I cried. "And I look horrible!"

At sixteen years old, I had a whopping 120 pounds on my 5 foot 7 inch frame. That was ten more pounds than I weighed in the fabulous pictures that filled my modeling portfolio. The traitorous pounds that made my face look puffy were keeping me from my dream of becoming a supermodel.

Every time I stepped on the scale it was torture. By any

normal person's standards, I would have been considered thin, but not by the fashion industry's standards and certainly not by the standards of my New York agent, Eileen Ford. After a weeklong fast, I walked into the agency and said, "Eileen, look. I've lost weight!" I weighed 118 pounds. She looked me over and said bluntly, "You're still fat—lose five more pounds."

My eating habits were out of control. The more I tried to lose weight, the more I ate. I bought Häagen-Dazs ice cream and consoled myself with it. I would eat an entire box of Frosted Flakes and a gallon of ice cream at one sitting. Then I would take a handful of laxatives. I sat with my head over a toilet trying to make myself vomit. I took diet pills to help me lose weight, speed up my system, and diuretics to rid myself of unwanted water. I wanted to look perfect, but my eating habits continued to spin out of control and so did my life. I could only be as happy as I was thin.

My looks consumed me. I was obsessed with food. When I scrutinized my appearance, I saw myself through a fun-house mirror. My view was distorted—what was real was not what I saw. Somewhere along the way, I had lost sight of what was true. When I looked in the mirror, I no longer saw the image of someone like Cheryl Ladd, but of Miss Piggy. My value, both to myself and to my agents, was in the way I looked, and since I could not look "perfect," I felt worthless.

During the next two years, I travelled 75,000 miles as a fashion model. I used food, alcohol, drugs, and men to try to fill an empty place in my life. The glamour and excitement of my life wore off quickly. I explored various churches and new-age philosophies, read self-help books, and consulted my horoscope daily—searching for answers, but I didn't find any. My weight roller-coastered from high to low, as did my emotions.

At the ripe old age of eighteen—when most young girls would have just graduated from high school and were just beginning their lives—I concluded that my life was over. Suicide seemed to be my only option. I flew home from Switzerland, to say good-bye to my family before I killed myself.

Soon after I reached home, a friend of mine called and invited me to church. The pastor asked, "Do you have a void in your life? Have you tried everything, but still feel empty?" It felt as through he was speaking directly to me. He shared about the Lord and how to receive His salvation. I ran forward, knelt down, and accepted the Lord that night, and my life took a new direction. My heart filled to overflowing. God healed me—physically and emotionally.

Ten years later, I attended a ladies' event at my church. My husband stayed home with our four young children. During the message, the speaker recalled: "I took my teenage daughters to

Disneyland. While we were waiting in line, I asked them to look around at the crowd and pick out a woman that they thought was beautiful. They couldn't find one."

As soon as I got home, I sat down in front of my computer and began writing about a life I hadn't talked about in years. I wondered, *Can I teach my children to see themselves through God's eyes?* I didn't want them to compare themselves with the media's impossible standards of beauty they saw on commercials, billboards, and magazine covers all around them. Would they realize that their worth to God was not measured by their weight or contingent upon high-chiseled cheekbones? How would I balance that message with the fact that they should take good care of the unique and wonderful bodies God created for them? As I tucked their sweet, pajama-clad bodies into bed that night, I read them a verse from First Samuel: "For the Lord does not see as man sees; for man looks at the outward appearance, but the Lord looks at the heart" (16:7 NKJV).

Over the years, I have encouraged my children to be beautiful—on the inside. My grown daughters now attend Bible college. They've been to Europe too—but as missionaries, not fashion models. My two sons grow taller by the day.

Recently, I awoke during the night, unable to sleep. It was

cold outside, but I was warm in my cozy bed as I lay next to my husband. With his arm draped across my body, he was so close that I could feel his heartbeat and his warm breath upon my face. I was filled with peace and contentment. Had I taken my life in that lonely hotel room twenty-two years ago, I would have missed all of this.

I still struggle sometimes with wanting to look younger and thinner. I wish that my stomach did not lie next to me when I sleep on my side! Fortunately, I know that physical beauty is only skin-deep and temporary, and that true beauty is soul deep. God accepts me regardless the size of my jeans, the condition of my skin, or my reflection in a mirror. He loves me so much that He sent His only Son to die for me. And I am, indeed, valuable to Him.

FALLING IN LOVE AGAIN

KATHRYN LAY

*Therefore shall a man leave his father and his mother, and shall
cleave unto his wife: and they shall be one flesh.*

GENESIS 2:24

"THE CHRISTIAN IS SUPPOSED TO LOVE HIS NEIGHBOR. AND SINCE HIS WIFE IS HIS NEAREST NEIGHBOR. SHE SHOULD BE HIS DEEPEST LOVE."

Martin Luther

After sixteen years of marriage, I fell head-over-heels in love.
How wonderful to fall in love and feel the joy of knowing
that this is the one God has chosen as your life partner. Your
heart beats quicker when you see him. You cherish the times
you are together, the times you laugh, pray, and plan together.

But what if it's the second time around? And what if the
one you've fallen head-over-heels in love with this second time
is your husband?

One of my favorite love songs is an oldie: When I Fall in
Love. It was playing as I walked down the aisle at my
wedding...the second one. At both wedding ceremonies in my
life, I met the same wonderful man at the front of the church.

Both times, I gave my heart, my commitment, and my promises to the same person.

Recently, my husband and I renewed our wedding vows. It wasn't on our 20th, 25th, or 50th anniversary like many couples choose to do. We did it sixteen years, three months, and twenty-two days after the first time.

Why?

We fell in love again—head-over-heels, heart-pounding, nerve-tingling love. God gave our marriage a high-voltage charge, and it is now stronger than ever.

We've always had what I considered an outstanding marriage. After all, we were still together after sixteen years, although seven out of nine couples in our immediate family had separated or divorced.

Unlike others, we began our marriage with two things in our favor. We both had a personal relationship with God, and we went through outstanding premarital counseling. As many of our friends' marriages began to shatter into thin shards of lost dreams, we remained together.

Our marriage weathered lost jobs, enormous financial difficulty, in-law problems, and ten years of sorrow-filled infertility.

As our sixteenth anniversary approached, we were still together—and even happy. We didn't have devastating fights.

We didn't have bitter secrets. Yet, something was missing. Something I felt God wanted us to have.

I went through a brief period of depression, irritated that my husband didn't know what I needed without having to tell him, yet not willing to tell him myself. Finally, once I saw that he noticed my coldness, I wrote a long letter relating my hurts and sorrows, and my frustration that he spent more time and effort on his ministry and his teaching than he did with me.

After the letter, as our daughter napped, we talked. I expected to hear deep-felt apologies, but instead received an explanation that some of my past attitudes and angry responses had caused him to pull away from me.

More hurt than ever, I went to the bathroom to cry.

Soon afterward, we sat together again on the couch, holding one another as he told me how he had prayed while I cried. Once he admitted his own feelings, the walls came down.

Changes in him had really begun a few weeks before while at a men's Promise Keepers' Conference. He had asked God what he was to take away from the conference and felt God whisper, "I want you to fall in love with your wife again."

From that day on, our relationship grew. As I thought over the steps that began with that first discussion, I realized there were five ways that we came to experience a renewed love.

First, we reevaluated our relationship. What kind of

marriage did we want? We knew we didn't want one like that of our parents and siblings, which often deteriorated into accusations, surface communication, abuse, or neglect. Our goal had always been to have a Christ-centered marriage, to be partners, not separate individuals who lived in our own worlds and occasionally came together. We didn't want just a good marriage. We both wanted a great one that would last.

We did expect occasional disagreements or conflicts, hurts, or miscommunication. We both knew that to have a great marriage meant hard work. We saw where we had grown lazy and taken one another for granted. Yet, we also saw how well our partnership worked, how much we truly enjoyed spending time together and had always been open in talking about our dreams, fears, and joys.

After that, we did the hardest thing, but it truly moved us forward. We released our past hurts and disappointments. A new Sunday school class we were involved in helped us do this. As if a gift from the Lord, the class began just a few days after our renewal began.

We used a workbook, *Building Your Marriage,* by Dennis Rainey. It required a commitment of a date night, a time to answer the questions from each chapter.

Sometimes they were difficult questions to answer and even more difficult to hear the answers from the other. Yet our honesty broke down any remaining bricks in the wall we'd built over the last few years.

We then made a decision to recommit ourselves to our marriage. We spent less time in the evenings watching television after our five-year-old went to bed, and more time talking about our day and the events in our lives.

As a result, our discussions became deeper, our prayer time stronger, and our intimacy more beautiful. We had an intense desire to be together as friends, lovers, and partners.

The closer we became, the more we worked at rejuvenating romance in our marriage. The closeness we shared in our talks and prayers led us to fall more deeply in love.

I remember, a few weeks after the changes began, running errands while my daughter was in preschool, and anticipating a date night I wanted to surprise Richard with that evening.

I felt like a school girl, my stomach in knots of excitement. I had always loved having my husband home, but suddenly, I couldn't wait to see him again. It wasn't a clingy feeling, but a true joy at the thought of seeing him again each afternoon.

As our sixteenth anniversary neared, we made plans to spend the weekend away. That first night, we went to dinner at a romantic, candle-lit Italian restaurant. Richard had always worried over gifts he'd given me for Christmas and birthdays, yet this time, he was excited and anxious for me to open my anniversary gift.

I stared at the beautiful diamond ring.

"There's more," he said.

While I looked through the box for matching earrings, he told me how he'd always loved me and would marry me all over again. Then, holding my hand, he asked, "Will you?"

I listened in surprise as he explained how he had spoken to our pastor about renewing our vows, found a best man, and talked to a fellow teacher who sang professionally. He wanted to invite all our friends and have them share in our recharged love.

Since the renewal of our relationship began months ago, we have continued to rejoice in one another. We cannot say we've never had minor disagreements or disappointments in something we've done or said, but there is a constant realization that God loved us so much that He brought us to one another.

I've come to understand what a gift marriage is from the Lord, and how special it is when we view our mate with this in mind. How exciting it is to see that God presented Eve to Adam and that the gift pleased Adam.

In my husband's vows to me during the renewal ceremony, he said, "God searched the world until He found the perfect mate for me. The perfect friend and partner. And He found you."

God opened the floodgates and renewed our marriage. As we stood before our friends and family who witnessed our commitment, I looked into my husband's eyes and saw how much God truly loved me.

Our first wedding was color-coordinated, well-planned, and rehearsed. Yet this one meant far more. For now, after sixteen years of knowing everything about one another, we were ready to say, "Yes, we made the right decision to marry then, and now, and forever."

This time, I fell in love with my eyes completely open. And the falling in love continues.

THE CAMPING ADVENTURE

TONYA RUIZ

"LOVE,
HONOR,
AND
NEGOTIATE."

Alan Loy McGinnis

Love suffers long and is kind; love does not envy; love does not

parade itself, is not puffed up; does not behave rudely, does not seek

its own, is not provoked, thinks no evil; does not rejoice in iniquity,

but rejoices in the truth; bears all things, believes all things, hopes

all things, endures all things. Love never fails.

1 CORINTHIANS 13:4-8 NKJV

"Pumpkin, I've got good news. We're going camping!" My husband of only three months excitedly informed me. Dread quickly overwhelmed me. "But Ron," I told him, "I've never camped before."

"Don't worry, Sugar. I'll take care of everything," he promised. "Look," I sweetly said, "in my family 'roughing it' meant sleeping with a window open at the Hilton." We both laughed. I was dead serious.

For weeks he shopped and packed. I had never seen him so enthusiastic about anything. On the appointed departure date, we drove off with our camping gear tied atop our white Ford Escort. He was smiling.

I was in charge of reading the map and only three hours into our journey we were lost. "Okay," I said, "Don't get frustrated. I'm doing the best I can. Which way is east again?" "Sugar pie," he patiently explained pointing with one hand and driving with the other, "North, south, east, and west. Didn't you take geography in school?" "Sure," I said, "and I got an A." He rolled his eyes as if that were impossible to believe, pulled the car over to the side of the road, and took the map out of my hands. Immediately, he solved the problem. "It would have been easier to follow," he scolded, "if you hadn't been holding it upside down."

Tired and weary, we finally reached our planned camping site. "When you get away from the city lights it sure is dark," I commented as we looked up at the stars in the sky. "I keep hearing scary noises." "Don't be silly, we're out in the middle of nowhere. Do you think a chainsaw murderer would come all the way out here?" "Of course not," I lied.

At sunrise, he walked to the lake to do some fishing, and I headed to the showers. Upon returning to our campsite he found me in the tent crying. "Why aren't you cleaned up, yet?" he inquired. "There are bats hanging from the ceiling in the shower." I sobbed. "They won't bother you, " he tried to comfort me.

The second night it rained and our air mattress turned into a life raft. We decided to move to a new location.

Ron drove to a scenic spot by a stream for our picnic. It was warm in the sun, and I decided that a dip in the water would refresh me. Slowly, I began to wade into the stream. Snakes, snakes, and more snakes gathered around me, their beady eyes watching my every move. I screamed and quickly learned to walk on water. Once on the bank, I screamed even louder for Ron. Upon close inspection, he assured me, "Nothing to worry about, those are just little water snakes."

We stopped the car and pulled over, looking for a place to pitch our tent. Ron liked it, "Look, Honey, we can camp here on the hill, and in the morning I can catch you breakfast from that stream." Either I was dizzy or the ground was moving. After my eyes adjusted, I realized the ground was blanketed with amphibians. "Don't worry, those newts are just migrating," he said. I ran for the car, and Ron followed. "I will not sleep with those things crawling all over me. Get me a hotel room, or take me home!"

After finding the only lodging within a hundred miles, Ron

rented a little cabin for us. *Well,* I consoled myself, *it may look slightly rustic, but at least I won't be sleeping with the newts.* Ron went out to collect kindling for the fireplace, the shack's only redeeming feature. I decided to crawl into bed to get warm, only to find it was already occupied by dozens of tiny arachnids. I took the pillow, brushed them away, and crawled in.

The bear's visit to our porch didn't scare me too much. He made a lot of noise, but I knew he wanted the outdoor trash can instead of me. At least the cabin had a locked door.

Around two in the morning, I heard scurrying. I tiptoed over to the light. When I turned it on, mice ran in every direction. I jumped onto the bed. Ron awoke with a start and reached for his hunting rifle. "What in the world is wrong?" "Mice," I whimpered as I sat in the middle of the bed, my head covered with the blanket. "Don't worry, they won't get on the bed," he said, before he resumed his snoring. I shook him awake, "I thought you were Prince Charming, but I was wrong. You're Grizzly Adams!" He pulled me under the covers and nuzzled me with his beard.

"I just don't get it, " he said over breakfast. "What more could you want? Fresh air, peace and quiet, and mountain streams full of trout?" He was invigorated by the adventure, but I was deflated. "We should have discussed this in premarital counseling," I said. "I love you, but a lifetime is going to be a long time if camping is involved!"

Grizzly said, "I have a solution." We drove into town, and he bought a lawn chair that he dubbed, "The Queen's Throne." He found a perfect spot next to a lake, put my chair in the sun with his manly camping chair next to it. "I am not putting that worm on the hook," I complained as he taught me how to fish. At dusk we headed back to town. "I won't tell anyone that my trout were bigger than yours," I promised. After a lovely dinner at a restaurant and hot showers at our hotel, I told Ron, "If you still want to 'rough it,' I could open a window." We both laughed.

Our twenty-year marriage has been a lot like that first camping trip. Learning to give and take, and working together to find solutions to challenges. There have been good years and bad years, but we've survived. Last year, we found a great compromise—a beautiful cabin near a lake and across the street from a day spa! Other than the moth invasion and a mouse incident, it was an almost perfect vacation.

MENDED MARRIAGE

SUSY DOWNER

Therefore, if anyone is in Christ, he is a new creation;

the old has gone, the new has come!

2 CORINTHIANS 5:17 NIV

"MARRIAGE IS LIKE TWIRLING A BATON, TURNING HANDSPRINGS, OR EATING WITH CHOPSTICKS; IT LOOKS SO EASY TILL YOU TRY IT."

Helen Rowland

I grew up in the Midwest with a warm, loving family. Active in church, we never thought of being anywhere else on a Sunday. But something happened when I was only fifteen months old that helped shape my character for the rest of my life.

I contracted eczema, a skin disease that looks worse than poison ivy and itches continually. I lost all my hair and had to wear mittens to keep me from tearing my skin. As I grew older, I couldn't play outside because perspiration made me itch more. I didn't sleep through the night until I was four. Night after night, Mom talked to me to keep my mind off the itching.

While this may sound like a calamity, in reality it made me

grow up—fast. Mom's nighttime conversations helped me mature rapidly. So did the avid reading I enjoyed in my time alone.

I became so self-confident that when a woman instinctively pulled her child away in an elevator, I said, "Don't worry. It's just eczema and it's not contagious."

My parents perceived me as unusually responsible, and allowed me to make key decisions at a young age. When I was only twelve, I began a swimming program in our backyard pool that eventually grew from four students to seventy by the time I graduated from high school.

The summer following my freshman year of high school I decided I wanted to be a lawyer. Though female vocational aptitude wasn't fashionable at that time, I never deviated from my goal. Every day confirmed my belief that I was in total control of my life. My plans included graduation from college and law school before I would marry.

Then I met Phil. When we fell in love, I rationalized away my previously set time schedule. He seemed like the perfect man. Funny and relaxed, he loved me with all his heart. He loved to discuss weighty issues. And he did not think it ridiculous that I wanted to go to law school, like most other men I had dated.

We married in 1971 after our junior year of college and

decided to take a semester off to camp in Europe. What could be more romantic than to spend four months in Europe without a care in the world? It was perfect.

That is, until the second day when Phil misplaced something; it sent him into a rage. He screamed and yelled. I tried to reason with him, and when that failed, I burst into tears. I cried myself to sleep that night. No one had ever yelled at me before. I wondered, *Who is this man that I've married?*

A pattern developed. Trifling irritations would trigger Phil's temper. He would yell and storm around, blaming me for whatever upset him. I would talk and reason with him and eventually cry.

My tears seemed to trigger a calm within him. He would profusely apologize and promise never to do it again. But he seldom went more than a few days without a blowup.

These confrontations left me physically and emotionally exhausted. His penitent attitude was the only thing that kept me going. As the days of arguments turned into weeks and the weeks into months, my love for Phil began to slowly slip away. Secretly I set a deadline in my mind. If things didn't improve by a certain date, it was over.

Not all of our times together were bad. We had some enjoyable experiences that eased the pressure as we entered law school. We especially loved going to class and studying for exams together.

We even argued as moot court partners. Once we had a legal brief due at 8:00 A.M. and had to stay up all night to finish it. Just before dawn, I told Phil I was sleepy and had to go to bed for an hour. He told me I couldn't because we wouldn't finish in time. I went to bed anyway.

After an hour, he awakened me and we began again. Phil dictated while I typed. As the clock neared the magic hour, I realized we weren't going to finish. I began to tell him how sorry I was when I noticed a twinkle in his eye.

"What is it?"

"Well, I just let you sleep for a minute and moved all the clocks forward an hour before I awakened you." I was so grateful to have that extra hour that I couldn't get upset with him!

Despite the fights, there were enough of the good times that I extended my deadline each time as the date neared. Eventually I reasoned that once we graduated from law school, Phil would relax.

About three years into our marriage, I met a woman named Liane at a baby shower, who exhibited an unusual peace. Despite some incredibly harsh circumstances in her life, she told me that she was so calm because she knew that God could handle any problem. At first that sounded inviting, but it didn't take long to reject the idea. No one could handle my life better than I could—including God.

I thought my job at Delta in corporate law, securities, and personnel work would be the answer to my problems. I loved my exciting, fulfilling career, and Phil had landed a great position with a growing firm. We were both grateful to work after so many years of school.

Our fights continued despite the so-called security, a new home, and the ability to travel just about anywhere thanks to my employer. They continued to follow the same pattern that had developed early in our marriage: Phil's yelling, my tears, our discussion, and his promise never to do it again.

How long could it continue? I wondered. *How many times could I push back my self-imposed deadline?* Fortunately, I never found out. Thanks to a Bible study I eventually began with Liane, a sweet woman I had met at a baby shower, and a women's retreat I attended soon after, life changed.

On that retreat I realized for the first time that it was possible to have a personal relationship with Jesus Christ. Woman after woman spoke about a living, loving God who wanted to have that kind of relationship with me.

As I considered their claims, I had to face the fact that I wasn't a Christian. I may have grown up in church and I still attended services half-heartedly, but I had never accepted

Christ. Yet, I wasn't willing to give up my sacred independence.

I'll never forget when Phil first heard the claims of Christ at a Christian businessmen's meeting. He then went on a retreat where he accepted Jesus as Savior and Lord. We had a great week without the typical fights and the following Sunday went to church together.

After church, I made dinner, and we sat down to eat in front of the television. That was a habit from law school days, when study breaks consisted of dinner with the evening news.

This afternoon I must have said something that triggered his temper. I saw that familiar look of rage cross his face. As he raised his fist over that last, "quivering" TV table, a familiar feeling returned. (He had smashed all of them with his fist during previous fights.) I thought sarcastically, *Well, this changed life really lasted a long time.*

Suddenly Phil stopped with his fist in mid air and said, "I'm going to go into the bedroom to pray. And I'm going to come back happy." When he did, the miracle overwhelmed me.

A verse I had heard in the Bible study with Liane immediately came to mind: "Therefore, if anyone is in Christ, he is a new creation; the old has gone, the new has come!" (2 Corinthians 5:17, NIV).

As Liane continued to disciple me, I watched Phil gradually

get a grip on his temper. While I continued to study the Bible and fellowship with other committed Christians, I realized how much God loved me. I finally admitted that whatever plan He had for my life would be better than anything I could plan myself.

Finally I said a simple prayer, telling God I understood my pride and independence were great hindrances in my life. Confessing that, I told Him I wanted to change and follow His ways instead of my own.

For the first time, I knew the reality of the Lord Jesus living in me. I found a new peace and direction, one that has remained with me to this day.

Now that Phil and I were both Christians, we lived happily ever after, right? Only in Hollywood! I realized that all those years of battle had killed the love I once felt for him.

I knew it was wrong to leave but I wanted to just the same. I didn't think I could spend my whole life with someone I didn't love. But Liane had taught me well, and I began to pray. I told the Lord, *You can do anything. Please, make me fall in love with Phil again.*

God is so good. He answered that prayer completely. As we prayed together and grew in our newfound faith, I developed a love for my husband that far surpassed the superficial feelings that first led me to marry him—because this love was a direct gift from God. I marveled at how Phil seemed to grow sweeter and more loving each day.

Looking back at how we have grown ever closer amid the challenges of raising six children, I can confidently say God is the greatest marriage mender. He took pieces we'd torn apart and mended them to produce a unique and beautiful masterpiece.

$\mathscr{S}$TANDING FOR WHAT I BELIEVED

JULIE JENKINS

I am the resurrection, and the life.

JOHN 11:25

"FAITH IS BELIEVING IN THINGS WHEN COMMON SENSE TELLS YOU NOT TO."

George Seaton

I awoke early one November day wrapped in romantic thoughts. David and I had been married less than two months, and it was thrilling to open my eyes and find my handsome 35-year-old husband doing his warm-up exercises beside the bed before his daily run. He leaned down, kissed me, and slipped one of his two dog-tag chains around my neck.

"Wear these till I come home," he whispered before he left.

David was a major in military intelligence at Fort Huachuca, Arizona, and as I fingered his tags around my neck, I thanked God for bringing us together. Our marriage was the second for both of us; one we had long prayed about.

I glanced at the clock, jumped up and showered. I had

joined a Red Cross class, and was training to become a volunteer at the post dental clinic. Before leaving for class, I wrote David a love note. While I taped it on the bathroom mirror, where he would see it when he came home to shower, I heard the wail of sirens. I paused to pray for whomever was injured, as I had done since I was a little girl. Then I went off to class, not realizing I had just prayed for my own husband.

I was in class when David's commanding officer appeared at the doorway and motioned for me to come into the hall. One look at his face told me something was wrong. He gave me the news as calmly as he could: "David was hit by a car while he was jogging."

As the colonel walked with me to the hospital adjacent to the dental clinic, I learned that David had been struck by a car traveling about 55 miles an hour. The driver had been temporarily blinded by the rising sun, and David had been thrown onto the hood, landing against the windshield. When the horrified driver hit his brakes, David had been catapulted some 64 feet and landed headfirst on the pavement.

When we reached the hospital, medics were moving him onto a flight for the University Medical Center (UMC) in Tucson, seventy-five miles away. I was in a state of shock while the colonel's wife drove me there.

At UMC's emergency room I was told David would be

taken to surgery to repair his broken legs and arm. But then a neurosurgeon appeared and canceled those plans. David's head scans revealed he had suffered multiple skull fractures, and little brain activity was detected. They would have to put in a shunt immediately to relieve pressure on his brain, and use a monitor to gauge his intracranial pressure moment by moment.

The neurosurgeon looked directly into my face. "Your husband is dying," he said. "He has two to forty-eight hours, at most."

I wanted to scream at him or ask if he could be wrong. But I had always been too polite to question people in authority. That's what Holleigh, my 21-year-old daughter from my previous marriage, said anyway. She always told me to stand up for myself. But the doctor towered over me now. "You should call your family and get them here fast," he was saying. "And I see your husband marked 'donor' on his driver's license, so you'll need to think about donating his organs."

Suddenly the room seemed to be closing in. I had to get outside. "Thank you," I said. "Excuse me. I have to go pray now." I stumbled to a patio and sank down onto a bench. How can this be happening? How can David be dying?

My mind escaped to the previous June, to the tranquil front porch of my lakefront house in Sackets Harbor, New York, where David and I had met. I lived a quiet life with Holleigh, and David was on a four-month assignment in the area. I sat reading my Bible on the front porch as David ran by each morning. One day he stopped and started a conversation about the Bible, which led to dating and a marriage proposal soon afterward. We both recognized each other as God's answer to our prayers for lifetime mates.

By the time David's father, mother, and brother, Mark, arrived at the hospital, I was fasting and praying—sometimes silently, sometimes murmuring softly into David's ear while I held his hand—hour by hour. A kind neurosurgeon, Dr. William D. Smith, was now on David's case, but the prognosis was still bleak. When doctors shone a light in David's eyes, there was no response. Soon David sank into a coma.

The pressure on David's brain shot up to five times above normal the next day. Dr. Smith explained that since the brain was swelling and pushing against the skull, circulation was cut off; my husband's brain was experiencing damage to such an extent that, if he lived, he would be a vegetable.

Forty-eight hours passed. Dr. Smith told us the monitor showed pressure on the brain that was incompatible with life. "Clinically, your husband is brain dead," he explained gently.

On the fifth day after the accident, when David's condition did not change, well-meaning friends drew up a list of how his organs could be used to help those in dire condition.

Arrangements were made for David to be buried in Arlington National Cemetery. I understood the others' motivation. I had put my husband in God's hands and would accept whatever happened. But I couldn't shake the feeling that neither God nor I was ready to give him up.

That evening, December 4, Dr. Smith called the family together. Gently but firmly he explained that we could continue to keep David on life-support indefinitely or we could make the decision to harvest his organs. Holleigh joined us as the family talked it over into the night, our hearts breaking.

When I went to my room, I felt lower than ever. Tears streamed down my face. I took my Bible to bed with me. *God, if David is truly dead, I understand. But if there's something more I should do, please let me know.*

I opened my Bible to the book of John and there was the story of Lazarus. I had read it many times before, but suddenly the words took on new meaning. Martha's brother, Lazarus, had been dead for four days when Jesus went to the tomb with Martha. As I read, my tears stopped abruptly. "I am the resurrection and the life," Jesus said, "he who believes in me, though he die, yet shall he live...Do you believe?" (John 11:25-26 RSV).

I sat up in bed. "Yes, I believe!" I said aloud. "I believe You can save David now just as You saved Lazarus then!"

The next morning I dressed in the brightest-colored clothes I had, as a symbol of life. Carrying my Bible as if it were a sword, I went into David's room to battle for his life. As usual, he was lying spread-eagle on that strangely shaped bed, which moved constantly to stimulate his circulation.

Maneuvering carefully around all the tubes and medical apparatuses, I began to read the eleventh chapter of John, standing over David's head, then on one side of him, then on the other, and at his feet, even kneeling and leaning under his bed. I was not trying to perform some magical ritual. Rather, I wanted to cover David's body with the Word of God. Doctors and nurses gave me sidelong glances—a few openly disdainful, a few embarrassed, and a few understanding. But I wasn't timid. I read aloud confidently.

When I had finished reading, I opened my Bible and laid it on David's chest—the same Bible that had attracted David to me in Sackets Harbor. With my hands on his head, I prayed aloud for a miracle, heedless of the medical people looking on. While I sang "Amazing Grace," David's favorite hymn, his father stood by the window, his hands clasped in prayer, and his brother, Mark, prayed in the chapel. Medical teams came and went.

A neurosurgeon stopped me in the hall afterward. "Get a grip on reality," she said. "Stop talking about miracles!"

For someone usually so awed by authority, I wasn't the slightest bit intimidated. "Our God is a mighty healer," I replied simply. When anyone referred to David as brain dead, I was surprised at the authority in my voice when I gave them the same response. Reports of others praying for David bolstered me even more. When I went to the hotel that night I slept peacefully.

The next day as I walked into David's room, his father met me at the door. "Don't get your hopes up," he said. "But when they examined David's eyes today they saw a flicker of response."

We sat watching and praying at David's bedside. As the hours passed, his arms moved, then later, his legs. On December 7, I wrote in my diary while sitting at David's side: "Buzzers and beeps resound in my husband's room—signs of life to all who hear that Jesus Christ is the healer!"

Gradually David responded more and more to what was going on around him. He woke up. He couldn't talk because he had a tube in his throat, so he wrote notes to his family clustered around his bed. With a shaky hand, he scrawled out to me: "I love you."

The neurosurgeons were astounded by the reversal of David's condition. They said they had never seen anyone so badly injured return to normal. Dr. Smith said he had never seen a miracle, but he thought he was seeing one now. When the tube was removed from David's throat, he murmured that I was beautiful and asked me to marry him. "We are married," I said, laughing for the first time in days. On December 8, doctors repaired the breaks in David's legs and arm. Shortly after, David was moved to the Tucson Veterans Administration Medical Center.

Day by day, little by little, his memory returned—starting with his earliest behavior and progressing onward. David fast-forwarded in a matter of days from childhood (where he used crayons and played with little cars), through high school and into college (where he sang the Indiana University anthem) to adulthood, where he regained most of his intellectual capacity.

As Holleigh and I helped David get ready to go home on February 2, a new nurse inadvertently placed his legs in an awkward position in the wheelchair. I politely but firmly corrected her, and my daughter smiled. "I'm proud of you, Mom," Holleigh said later. "You stand up for yourself these days."

I fingered the dog tags around my neck, the ones I had never removed. Yes, I had stood up for what I believed in. And now my husband was coming home.

A MARRIAGE MADE IN HEAVEN

KAREN R. KILBY

Love is patient and kind. Love is not jealous or boastful or proud or rude. Love does not demand its own way. Love is not irritable, and it keeps no record of when it has been wronged. It is never glad about injustice but rejoices whenever the truth wins out. Love never gives up, never loses faith, is always hopeful, and endures through every circumstance. Love will last forever.

1 CORINTHIANS 13:4-8 NLT

"A WEDDING ANNIVERSARY IS THE CELEBRATION OF LOVE, TRUST, PARTNERSHIP, TOLERANCE, AND TENACITY. THE ORDER VARIES FOR ANY GIVEN YEAR."

Paul Sweeney

We sat across the kitchen table from each other, not quite knowing what to say. We had just come from a counseling session with the pastor of a local church. It was my hope that if anyone had the answer to saving our marriage, it would be God, and just maybe this pastor could lead us to Him. The pastor's advice was exactly what I had expected: If we trusted

193

God to be a part of our marriage, He would help us overcome our differences. "Well," David said to me when we got home, "you're the one with the connection to God." Then he got up from the table and left for work.

Connected to God, I thought. How good it felt to be connected to God. I wanted to be connected to David also. We had been married for ten years and had four beautiful children and a lovely home. Anyone looking at us from the outside would have thought we had it all together. The truth of the matter was we were on the verge of a separation.

If it hadn't been for my friend, Marie, I wouldn't have known how to connect to God. We were in a book club together. One evening, Marie gave me a book to read that wasn't on the Book of the Month list. The author seemed to know everything about me although he had never met me. He told me about looking for fulfillment in all the wrong places and that the void in my life was actually a spiritual hunger to know God and bring me into a relationship with Him. How could this author know so much of what I was feeling, the recurring emptiness that could never be filled? It seemed that no matter what I did—having a family, working part-time, volunteer club work, decorating one home after another—nothing seemed to fill the void.

I had begun to think I had married the wrong man. I

understood that I wasn't perfect—who is? I thought the good I did would outweigh the bad. Now I was faced with God's truth, and I had a decision to make. As I struggled with this, a Bible verse came to mind. Jesus said, "I have come that you might have life and have it more abundantly" (John 10:10). That's what I wanted—a life that counted for something, full of promise and hope. I had no idea how it would happen, but I decided that this promise from God was better than anything I could plan on my own. God's peace flooded my heart. The emptiness I had felt was gone. I was actually content! I was at peace with myself and with God. Jesus had made the connection.

Until that moment, I had felt that David was responsible for making me happy. As a result, our relationship suffered as he became increasingly frustrated trying to please me without result. I still cared for David, but it was more like the love for a brother—my affections had waned toward him as a husband.

As I sat at the table, contemplating what David had said, the thought came to me that I should call him at work and say the words, "I love you." Where in the world did that thought come from? God must certainly know I didn't have those feelings—at the moment. The thought persisted—and it was as if God was telling me He would provide what I needed at just the right time. So I made the call, David's response was, "You don't know how much I needed to hear that." When I hung up

I thought, *That was great!* Then it hit me. David would be coming home at 5:00! Then what? At that moment I felt God prodding me to meet him at the door with a hug and a kiss, and again reminded me that He would give me what I needed at just the right time. And He did!

When I began to attend Friendship Bible Coffees through a Christian Women's Club, I learned the love passage that explained what God had been teaching me: "Love is patient and kind; never jealous or envious, never boastful or proud, never haughty, selfish, or rude. Love does not demand its own way. It isn't irritable or touchy. It doesn't hold grudges and will hardly even notice when others do it wrong. It is never glad about injustice, but rejoices whenever truth wins out. If you love someone, you will be loyal to him no matter what the cost. You will always believe in him, always expect the best of him, and always stand your ground defending him."

I understood, perhaps for the first time, that it wasn't what David could do for me but what God could do inside my heart. That was such a different way of living and loving from what I had ever experienced. I used to say, "Three strikes and you're out!" Now I was given a choice of how I could react and relate. I could choose to follow God's unconditional love for David or my natural instinct to be unforgiving and selfish.

David began to notice that the changes in me were real, and

he began to respond to God's love himself. The Bible says, "When someone becomes a Christian, he becomes a brand-new person inside. He's not the same anymore. A new life has begun." That's exactly what happened to me and to David.

Over the years, the strength of our love and faith in God has enabled us to face many difficulties: teenage rebellion, unemployment, a family member battling substance abuse, losing someone we loved to suicide, financial problems, and even David's heart attack. Yet in all of these situations, we found God to be trustworthy—believing that our security is in His hands, not just today but for all of our tomorrows.

A few years ago, we traveled to Spain to celebrate an anniversary. On one of our sightseeing trips, we went to the Rock of Gibraltar, a fortress that has stood in the Mediterranean Sea for centuries. It is the symbol Prudential Life Insurance uses to represent security and trust. As the road wound its way down toward the sea, suddenly the magnificent rock rose into view from miles away. It looked majestic— immovable. Every bit what you would expect a mighty fortress to be.

At that moment, I recalled a verse in the book of Psalms, "When my heart is faint and overwhelmed, lead me to the mighty towering rock of safety." Looking back I see that God's tender and watchful hand was guiding me—guiding us—to a stronger, solid, sustaining love. When all seemed a loss, it was God who became our towering rock and fortress of safety.

THE PARABLE OF THE COFFEE FILTER

NANCY C. ANDERSON

A soft answer turns away wrath, but a harsh word stirs up anger.

PROVERBS 15:1 NKJV

"STICKS AND STONES MAY BREAK OUR BONES, BUT WORDS WILL BREAK OUR HEARTS."

Robert Fulghum, All I Ever Needed to Know I Learned in Kindergarten

My brother Dan said, "I'm going home! Your bickering is driving me nuts. Your constant fighting wears me out."

I defended our behavior, "Hey, it's not like we disagree about everything. Ron and I agree on all the major issues. We hardly ever fight about big stuff like how to spend our money, where to go to church, or how to raise Nick. It's the little stuff that gets to us."

He sighed and said, "Well, I'm sick of hearing you go to war over where to put the towel rack, which TV shows to watch, or who's a better driver. It's all just dumb. None of it will matter a year from now. I can tell that Ron is really mad by the way he stomped up the stairs. Why did you have to criticize the way he mowed the lawn? I know it wasn't perfect, but couldn't you just let it go?"

"No," I replied. "We're having company tomorrow, and I want the yard to be perfect. So? I told him to fix it, big deal! And I won, because he went back out there and did the job right!"

Dan replied with a serious look on his face, "If you keep this up, you may win the arguments, but lose your husband."

I laughed and said, "Oh, stop being so melodramatic!"

The next evening, Ron and I went out to dinner with some friends we hadn't seen in several years. We remembered Carl as funny and outgoing, but he seemed rather quiet and looked exhausted. His wife, Beth, did most of the talking. She told us about her fabulous accomplishments and then endlessly bragged about her brilliant, Mensa-bound children. The only times she included Carl in the conversation were to criticize him.

After we ordered our dinner, she said accusingly, "Carl, I saw you flirting with that waitress!" (He wasn't.)

"Caarrrrlll," she whined, "can't you do anything right? You are holding your fork like a little kid!" (He was.)

When he mispronounced an item on the dessert menu, she said, "No wonder you didn't go to college, you can't read!" She laughed so hard at that that she snorted, but she was the only one laughing.

Carl didn't even respond. He just looked over at us with an empty face and a blank stare. Then he shrugged his drooping shoulders.

The rest of the evening became more oppressive as she continued to berate him about almost everything he said or did. I thought to myself, *I wonder if this is how my brother feels when I criticize Ron.*

We said good-bye to Beth and Carl and left the restaurant in silence. When we got in the car, I spoke first, "Do I sound like her?"

Ron said, "You're not that bad."

I asked, "How bad am I?"

"Pretty bad," he half whispered.

The next morning, as I poured water into the coffeepot, I looked over at my "Devotions for Wives" calendar. "The wise woman builds her house, but the foolish tears it down with her own hands," it read. *Or with her own mouth,* I thought.

"A nagging wife annoys like a constant dripping." How can I stop this horrible pattern?

"Put a guard over my mouth, that I may not sin with it." Oh, dear Jesus, show me how!

I carefully spooned the vanilla nut decaf into the pot as I remembered the day I forgot the filter. The coffee was bitter and full of undrinkable grounds. I had had to throw it away.

Then it dawned on me. The coffee, without filtering, is like my coarse and bitter speech. I prayed, "Oh, please Lord, install a filter between my brain and my mouth. Help me to choose my words carefully and use smooth and mellow language. Thank You for teaching me the 'Parable of the Coffee Filter.' I won't forget it."

An hour later, Ron timidly asked, "What do you think about moving the couch over by the window? We'd be able to see the TV better."

My first thought was to tell him why that was a dumb idea. *The couch will fade if you put it in the sunlight and besides, you already watch too much TV.*

But instead of my usual hasty reply, I let the coarse thoughts drip through my newly installed filter and calmly said, "That might be a good idea. Let's try it for a few days and see if we like it. I'll help you move it!"

He lifted his end of the sofa in stunned silence. Once we had it in place, he asked with concern, "Are you okay? Do you have a headache?"

I chuckled, "I'm great, Honey, never better. Can I get you a cup of coffee?"

THE HUMBUG HOLIDAYS AND THE LEAN-TO SNOWMAN

PATRICIA LORENZ

We depend on the Lord alone to save us.

Only he can help us, protecting us like a shield.

PSALM 33:20 NLT

"IN THE DEPTH OF WINTER I FINALLY LEARNED THAT THERE WAS IN ME AN INVINCIBLE SUMMER."

Albert Camus

I was going through the motions—everything a good mom is supposed to do before Christmas. I lugged out the boxes of holiday decorations. Baked my every-year-the-same-two-kinds of cookies. And even bought a real Christmas tree for a change.

I was going through the motions, but my heart was bogged down with a dull ache. I wasn't looking forward to Christmas one bit. My divorce had been finalized the past April, and my ex-husband was already remarried.

My oldest daughter, Jeanne, was in Yugoslavia for the year as a foreign exchange student and wouldn't be home for the holidays. This was the first time that all four of my children wouldn't be with me for Christmas. Plus the annual New Year's Eve get-together at my folks' house in Illinois had been canceled.

I was tired and grumpy. My job writing radio commercials at Milwaukee's biggest radio station became more hectic every day. Nearly every business in town wanted to advertise during the holiday season, and that meant longer and longer hours at work.

Then there was the real nemesis, holiday shopping, a chore I kept putting off. I was supposed to be planning and buying not only for my annual holiday party for the neighbors, but Andrew's eighth birthday on December 27, and Julia's seventeenth birthday on January 4 as well. How would I get through it all when "bah humbug" was on the tip of my tongue?

During the night of December 15, a snowstorm ripped through Wisconsin, dumping twelve inches of snow. Although Milwaukee is usually prepared for the worst, this blizzard finished its onslaught just before rush hour traffic, bringing the interstate highways to a standstill. The next day all the schools and most businesses were closed. Even the radio station where I worked, eighteen miles from my home, urged early-morning risers to stay in bed because the roads were impassable.

After viewing the picture-postcard scene outdoors, I forgot my down-in-the-dumps attitude, grabbed Andrew and said, "Come on, buddy, let's make a snowman!"

Andrew and I scooped up big handfuls of the wet, perfect-packing snow and built a base fit for a kingpin. Andrew rolled a ball of snow for the next level into such a huge mass that I had to get down on my hands and knees to shove it toward our mighty base.

When I hoisted Andrew's third boulder onto this Amazon snowperson, I felt like Wonder Woman pressing a hundred pounds. As our snowman reached a solid seven feet tall, I carefully placed Andrew's bowling-ball-sized snow head on top with the help of a stool.

"He needs a face, Mom." While I smoothed the snow and pounded arms and a waistline into our giant snowman, Andrew ran inside and returned with a silly beach hat with built-in sunglasses for eyes and a Superman cape that we plastered on the back of the giant.

Andrew and I stepped back to admire our noble snowman.

Straight and tall. Ruler of the yard. When I took their picture, Andrew's head barely reached the snowman's middle.

It was warmer the next morning, and when I looked outside the kitchen window I noticed that Super Snowman seemed to lean forward a little. I hoped he wouldn't fall over before Andrew got home from school that day.

Late that afternoon when I returned home after a hectic, make-up-all-the-work-from-yesterday, day at the radio station, I saw that our snowman hadn't fallen over, but leaned even farther forward at a very precarious forty-five-degree angle. His posture reminded me of the way I felt. Tired, crabby, out-of-sorts, and with the weight of the world on my shoulders.

The next morning Super Snowman continued so far forward that it almost seemed a physical impossibility. I had to walk out into the yard to see him up close. What on earth is holding him up? I wondered, absolutely amazed.

The Superman cape, instead of being around his neck, now dangled freely in the wind as old Frosty's bent chest, shoulders, and head were almost parallel to the ground.

My own shoulders sagged beneath the weight of depression each time I remembered that Christmas was almost here. A letter from Jeanne arrived saying that since Christmas wasn't a national holiday in Yugoslavia, she'd have to go to school on December 25. I missed Jeanne's smile, her wacky sense of humor, and her contagious holiday spirit.

The fourth day after we built the snowman was Saturday the nineteenth, the day I'd promised to take Andrew to Chicago on the train.

Andrew loved the adventure of his first train and taxi rides, the trip to the top of the world's tallest building, the visit to the Shedd Aquarium, and the toy departments of every major store on State Street. But I was depressed by the fact that it rained all day, that the visibility at the top of the Sears Tower was zero, and that the all-day adventure left me totally exhausted.

Late that night, after the two-hour train ride back to Milwaukee, Andrew and I arrived home, only to be greeted by the snowman, who by this time, after a warmer day of drizzling rain, was now totally bent over from its base and perfectly parallel to the ground...and yet still balanced six inches above the slushy snow.

That's me out there, I said to myself. About to fall face down into a snowbank. But why didn't our snowman fall? Nothing, absolutely nothing, supported the weight of that seven-foot-tall giant.

Just like there isn't anything or anybody supporting me during this awful holiday season, I blubbered mentally.

I wondered, *what had supported the snowman in such a precarious position? Was it God in His almighty power? A freak of nature? A combination of ice, wind, rain, and snow that had bonded to the mighty Super Snowman?* I had a feeling there was a lesson to be learned from watching his decline. The lesson came to me gradually during the next two weeks.

On Christmas Eve, at the children's insistence, we attended the family services at our parish church and dined on our traditional oyster stew afterwards. Then Andrew brought out the Bible for the yearly reading of the Christmas story before the children and I opened gifts.

Later we attended a midnight candle service with friends at their church and finally a phone call from Jeanne in Yugoslavia brimmed with good news of an impromptu Christmas celebration planned by the mother of the family she was staying with.

The next day some friends offered to co-host my big neighborhood party which turned into a smashing success. On December 27, Andrew was delighted with his three-person birthday party. The next weekend my out-of-town family got together for a long New Year's Eve weekend at my house, filling our home with the madcap merriment of ten houseguests who all pitched in to help with everything. And when Julia simplified another dilemma by saying that all she wanted for her birthday was a watch and "lunch out with

Mom," I smiled all day.

I learned that no matter how depressed, overwhelmed, saddened, lonely, or stressed out we become, there's always someone or something to help us find or recapture our own inner strength, just like there was for the falling-down, stoop-shouldered Super Snowman.

During his four-day lifespan, he showed me an amazing strength from within…a strength that came to me gradually, bit by bit, as each person in my life stepped up to boost my faith and my spirits to heavenly skies.

It was indeed a holiday season to cherish.

ℰMBRACED BY PRAYER

KATHLEEN KELLEY

Answer me when I call to you, O my righteous God. Give me relief from my distress; be merciful to me and hear my prayer.

PSALM 4:1 NIV

"LET ME NOT PRAY TO BE SHELTERED FROM DANGER, BUT TO BE FEARLESS IN FACING DANGER...."

Rabin dranath Tagore

I looked up at the snow-crowned peak of the Mount of the Holy Cross, stark and eerie in the light of dawn. The roughly five-mile zigzag trek from our base camp at 10,300 feet to the 14,005-foot summit included a special obstacle: a massive field of boulders, some of them taller than my five-foot frame. For a week my climbing partner, Jody, and I had hiked the mountains of Colorado to become acclimated to the altitude; I was ready for the challenge ahead.

My career as a physical education instructor and the demands of raising four kids kept me active most of my sixty-seven years. When my husband, Don, died in an automobile accident in 1986, my old life crumbled. But I continued to push forward, learning to be independent. Taking up climbing in 1990 was the first big step to mold a new Kathleen. I had twenty climbs behind me, including two up Mount Kilimanjaro.

I hoisted my pack—which held three water bottles, snacks, a whistle, a Mylar emergency blanket, and other essentials— and glanced at Jody. Though she was younger, we had about the same amount of climbing experience. I grinned at her, bundled in almost as many layers as I was. With my three waterproof jackets, gloves, sweatpants, and baseball cap, I was prepared for the chilly evening temperatures and sudden storms that could lead to hypothermia.

The July afternoon was bright, making every tree, rock, and wildflower stand out. I drank in the crisp air and thought of Don. In three days it would be the eleventh anniversary of his death, and yet it felt like just yesterday we walked through the woods by our summer cottage in Wisconsin. I always felt closer to him when I was close to nature.

By 1:00 P.M. Jody and I were at 12,000 feet, making good time. We kept a steady distance behind a couple of male climbers we had nicknamed "khaki pants" and "blue backpack." Then we hit the boulder field. It was hard to grasp the huge smooth rocks, and even harder to distinguish the cairns (marker rocks pointing out the trail). With each arduous step, I realized the descent would be that much more

treacherous. I lagged a good 200 yards behind Jody. I knew I
would never get to the top and back down by nightfall. I
leaned against a boulder to catch my breath, staring at my dirt-
spattered shoes. *Not going to make it this time,* Kathleen, I told
myself, breathing hard. I glanced up the mountain at Jody,
who had stopped. I waved her on. "You go. I'll be right here,"
I yelled and gestured. For the first time in the five years we
had climbed together, I wouldn't stand next to Jody on the
summit, taking in the view.

I settled down onto a tablelike boulder and rested, feeling
my heartbeat slow. I drank some water and wiped the sweat
off my neck and face. I dozed, then heard a rustle on the trail
above me. Turning, I saw "khaki pants," eyes intent on the
ground, navigating the boulders. Should I call out? I glanced at
my watch. *No need. Jody will be here soon and we'll go down
together,* I thought. At dusk I began scanning the mountain.
Where is she? I wondered, my shoulders tightening. I got up
and stretched, then sat again to wait for Jody.

She must have missed me, I finally told myself as a cloud
blanketed the moon. Well, I'll just walk down in the morning, I
decided. A cold raindrop brushed my ear and soon I was in the
midst of an icy shower. I nestled between two large boulders,
yanked down my cap and pulled my blanket close. Then I
drew my knees up to my chest, wrapped my arms around them

and fell into a fitful sleep.

The next morning I looked into the cloudless sky. I was on my own. Part of the adventure, I rallied myself. I got up and surveyed my surroundings. I checked my supplies. Then it hit me. Jody had our only map. Now what? I would have to make it down solo, but who better to rely on than myself?

I walked for two hours along the edge of the boulder field, carefully picking my way among the rain-slickened rocks. I had thought I had the hang of it, but then I slipped and my feet shot from under me. I landed hard on my backside and slid slowly, painfully down the mountain. I leaned back into my pack to keep from tumbling head over heels, but I continued to pick up speed, bouncing over the scree. Abruptly, I hit a tangle of bushes. I grabbed some branches and halted my slide, then crawled to a jutting rock shelf. The seat of my sweatpants was in shreds. I picked myself up, then turned around.

What I saw made me gasp. Above was a 45-degree slope the length of two football fields, littered with loose rock. Climbing it would be impossible. The only practical alternative was to stay put.

Strangely, I didn't feel panicked. Jody will have reached the bottom by now, I told myself. Help is on the way. I just have to wait.

I ate raisins. I watched the sun crawl across the sky.

Occasionally I blew my whistle. Around noon I took the last sip of water from the third bottle. In the distance to my right, a creek shimmered. Far above me, snow glistened like diamonds.

I settled down on a bed of pine brush for my second night on the mountain.

The next morning I braced myself against a rock and swung my stiff legs back and forth to circulate bloodflow. I was parched, but all I had left were my snacks. I unwrapped the peanut butter and jelly sandwich I planned for lunch the first day and took a bite. Without saliva, it was like trying to chew wood. I spit it out. I just had to have water. That afternoon it came.

The sky darkened rapidly. Lightning ripped the sky. I cupped the blanket on my lap to form a pool and plunged my face into the water, lapping it up like an animal. I collected pool after pool, directing each into a bottle. As the storm abated, I spied helicopters far overhead. Too far. Feeling giddy, I closed my eyes and drifted off.

"Kathleen."

I jerked my head up. Don? I extended my arms to him. My husband had come for me. With a start I opened my eyes and shielded my face from tiny hail pellets. "Don, I'm here!" I cried. A dream. But it had seemed so real! I rubbed my eyes and collapsed back onto the rock. I pulled the thin blanket over me, shivering and thought, *You have got to get off this mountain, Kathleen.*

The next morning I awoke feeling clammy and achingly alone. It was July 28, the eleventh anniversary of Don's death. In my mind I replayed our lives together: the way he gazed into my eyes at our first dance, the time he repainted a bedroom for Valentine's Day, how he held me after our youngest set out on her own. I smiled at the thought of his dresser drawers, neat enough to pass a military inspection; his strong hands polishing all the shoes in the household and lining them up at the top of the stairs; the silly songs he sang on family road trips. It was like watching a wonderful movie— until the tragic ending. Don could never have seen it coming: A boy adjusting his tape deck missed a stop sign and slammed into his car.

Now I, who had prepared meticulously for this climb, found myself stranded and helpless. Another senseless situation. I still felt amazingly calm and not especially weak, but I knew there was a limit to how long anyone could survive thirst, hunger, and exposure. Questions lingered in my thoughts, *Would I die on the same day as Don? Or would God help me to find my way as He had after Don's death?* I whispered a prayer to God and settled into my usual position, with my arms wrapped around my knees, and went to sleep.

The next morning the sun shone warmly and dried my clothes. I used safety pins to mend the tears in my pants and exercised the best I could.

I looked up. Helicopters! I grabbed my mirror and tried to catch the sunlight so I could use the reflection as a signal, but it was too small to do much good. I picked up my silvery blanket and waved it frantically. Throughout the day helicopters swooped nearby, only to rise again out of sight. My hopes sank with the sun into my fifth night on the mountain.

It was quiet the next morning, with no helicopters whirring overhead. *They've given up,* I thought. Still, I struggled to exercise my limbs. Then I heard a sound. I looked up. A helicopter was right above me. Within seconds I was lifted by a tall young man. "I've got you; you're okay now," he said.

I let myself go limp in his arms. It's over. I was rushed to Vail Valley Medical Center, where I was treated for dehydration and minor abrasions.

Jody was waiting for me. She had followed someone she thought was me—maybe "blue backpack"—out of the boulder field. People, dogs, and helicopter crews had combed the mountain for me, though no one had thought I could survive for six days. "Everyone said it was impossible," Jody told me.

I felt proud of myself—I had kept my cool. My training

and experience had paid off when it counted. But something nagged at me, as if there were more to it than that. When I flew home to St. Louis, I was greeted by a cheering throng carrying balloons, banners, and flowers. I rushed into my children's embraces. Relatives and friends told me over and over,

"I prayed for you."

Cards and letters from acquaintances and strangers filled my mailbox: "We prayed for you." People who recognized me from the media coverage said, "Hey, were you that lady on the mountain? I prayed for you." *Is that why I felt so calm?* I wondered.

A few days after I got home, my teenage godson Patrick visited me. "Weren't you scared?" he asked.

"No, I was wrapped in prayer," I said, putting my arms around myself. Suddenly I realized that was the same position I had sat in on the mountain. A feeling of warmth enveloped me, as if I were embraced at once by everyone who had prayed for me.

All along I was protected. It was the last piece of the puzzle.

Now when I go climbing, I still prepare meticulously, but I remember I am never truly on my own. God was there to guide me after I lost Don, and He was there to protect me when I was stranded. I'm proud of my self-sufficiency, but now I pay special attention to the prayers I and my loved ones offer to God—they are the most important supplies I carry.

HE ROSE

LINDA HENSON

Judge not, that ye be not judged.

MATTHEW 7:1

"NOTHING MAKES A WOMAN MORE BEAUTIFUL THAN THE BELIEF THAT SHE IS BEAUTIFUL."

Sophia Loren

I was permanently locked in the "fat girl" box—you know, the one the mime tries to get out of, but never can. I was seven the first time I was made aware that my weight made me somehow undesirable. My mother had made me a blue dress with a circular skirt and tiny ballerinas printed all over it. I thought it was the prettiest dress I had ever seen.

When that dress was pulled on over my head and the sash tied in the back, I was sure I looked like the beautiful dancers in the print. I couldn't wait to wear it to school. It was a dress that would usually have been kept in the far end of the closet for Sundays, but this week my mother was behind in the laundry, so she reluctantly let me wear it to school. I couldn't wait to show it off.

Before the bell rang—the signal for everyone to be in their seats, I twirled and twirled envisioning myself to be as beautiful as the ballerinas on my frock. A crowd of second graders gathered around me. I was on a cloud, knowing everyone around admired my dress and my prowess as a dancer.

But as I took one last whirl for a grand finale, a little boy in my audience said, "It's a pretty dress, but you're fat!" I could hear the low murmur of agreement, and then the crowd dispersed. My cloud of glory burst into the rains of doom and gloom. The dress, once such a delight, became a symbol of shame. I never wanted to wear it again. I walked in the front door after school and burst into tears. Of course, my mother comforted me and told me I wasn't fat, but the hard truth had already been spoken. Whatever I was, it wasn't beautiful.

That day marked the beginning. Every summer I spent a night with the "country" cousins on the farm. That branch on our family tree was very productive: There were six kids in the family and with no bathtub in the farmhouse, dirty faces were the usual look. There were cows and chickens to feed, and somehow a faint smell of the animals always seemed to find its way into the house. But the unkempt state of the household didn't seem to bother anyone. Free to go barefoot and play in the whitewashed milking barn brought endless hours of fun.

Everything went well until the older boys began to chat, "Fatty, fatty, two-by-four, Couldn't get through the bathroom door; so she did it on the floor, fatty, fatty two-by-four."

It was so humiliating; I wanted to go home.

Seventh-grade cheerleader tryouts were held in the fall. I was loud. I was a leader. Why not try out? My mistake. Each girl performed a cheer in front of the student body and then the students voted for their favorites. It didn't surprise me that I didn't win the competition; I had an idea that my size would be against me. But the real hurt came when friends told me the painful truth: I was actually the best cheerleader, it was just that...I was too fat.

Throughout high school my weight affected my social life. I never had a date. Fortunately, I had two wonderful best friends who were twins. They, too, had a problem with their weight, so we encouraged each other by ignoring our size and just enjoyed our teen years. We attended the same church and poured ourselves into the youth group activities. Unless someone pointed out our sizes, we didn't think about it. We used our energy to excel in school and became leaders of clubs and activities.

My senior year rolled around, and the twins, who were one year older, left for college. Suddenly there was a huge vacancy in my life. For the first time I didn't have anyone to hang out with. A boy who was a "social reject" in the teen circles began to ask me out. Any other time I would have refused, but I was lonely. At least he was someone to go to the movies with on Saturday nights.

Apparently, the stress of going out with anyone of the opposite sex affected me so much that I couldn't eat, and I began to lose weight! I couldn't believe it! Through the years I experimented with all kinds of diets and now, the weight just seemed to fall off. When graduation day arrived, I wore a size five.

By the time I went to college in the fall, I had a whole new wardrobe and as far as I could tell, my metabolism had changed. I could eat normally without gaining weight. The first day on campus I met a guy who seemed to be the man of my dreams, and two years later we married. He saw the "before" pictures of my early years and was glad he had met me "after." And I, too, was so thankful that the weight problem seemed to have vanished.

But the image of myself as an undesirable fat girl was seared into my mind. No matter my size, I wore shirts with the tail out or baggy clothes, trying to hide my body. Somewhere inside, I had a hard time believing that my husband really loved the fat, ugly girl I felt myself to be.

One Easter, our church invited an actor who portrayed Jesus to minister. The local ministers' group arranged a Good Friday service in the school gymnasium in order for the entire community to enjoy the performance. Our town was small and there were no motels, so we invited this man to stay in our home.

At the dinner table he began to tell us that as he presented Jesus' Sermon on the Mount, he would reach the passage about not judging, and present a visual scene. He would pick up a rose, walk into the audience, and hand it to the prettiest young woman he could see. People would "raise an eyebrow" at the thought of Jesus noticing a pretty girl! Then he would quote, "Judge not, that ye be not judged. For with what judgment ye judge, ye shall be judged." Wow! That would make a powerful point!

We arrived early at the gymnasium so that the actor could make his preparations. I herded my daughters up the bleachers and found a good seat about four rows up directly in front of the speaker's area. People filed in, clattered up the noisy wooden planks and nearly filled all of the seats. Everyone looked forward to such a different Good Friday service.

The leader of the local clergy group welcomed the crowd, made the necessary announcements, and then asked everyone to bow their heads and close their eyes in prayer. We were an obedient group, and the minister said his prayer. When it was time for the "amen," a different voice spoke. As we looked up, the minister was gone and "Jesus" was standing before us. A quiet gasp went through the crowd. A "holy hush" fell over the listeners.

"Blessed are the poor in spirit; for theirs is the Kingdom of heaven," he began his presentation of Jesus' words. As he stood before us in flowing robes, we felt we were hearing the sermon for the first time—and from the mouth of the original speaker. I waited with anticipation for the "judgment" verses. I looked around the crowd and wondered who he would pick for the presentation of the rose. Just behind me sat a beautiful girl with long blonde hair. She was the one, I was sure.

While I was still guessing, I saw him pick up the rose and move in our direction. I was right; he was headed for the girl behind me. I knew he would have to make his way by me to get to her, so I bent over and started to move my belongings, clearing a path. All of a sudden, as I looked down, I saw two feet in sandals stop before me. They were stationary, not moving on beyond me. My heart nearly stopped! For a moment I froze. Surely, he wasn't stopping in front of me! Slowly, I lifted my eyes up the white garments and there...I saw the hands of Jesus with the rose outstretched, presenting it to me! Filled with disbelief, I lifted my eyes to his face. No longer was this my newfound friend—it was Jesus! I began to melt. Tears flowed! I was beautiful to Him!

That experience crumbled the walls of the box that had entrapped me. For the first time I realized that the size or shape of my body was insignificant. I was beautiful to Jesus, and that made me acceptable. Seeing myself through the eyes of Jesus, I realized I was beautiful. He set me free from "the box" so that I could be all that He designed me to be.

IFTY FIFTY

PATRICIA LORENZ

Commit thy way unto the Lord; trust also in him;

and he shall bring it to pass.

PSALM 37:5

"THE BEST
BIRTHDAYS
OF ALL
ARE THOSE
THAT
HAVEN'T
ARRIVED
YET."

Robert Orben

"Come on, Mom, I'm really hungry for a big cheeseburger and fries! Can't we go out to eat?" my son, Andrew, implored.

"No. Fast food is too expensive. There is leftover meatloaf at home," I snapped.

Lately, as my fiftieth birthday loomed just over the horizon, I'd become a money-hoarding crab.

I'd loved my forties. They were fun, energetic, and full of life.

I'd accomplished a lot. A month before I turned forty I became a single parent to my four children, but thanks to team effort and lots of prayer, we survived the next decade beautifully. I managed the three oldest through their teenage years without too many new gray hairs, and they were now college graduates living on their own and supporting themselves with interesting careers. I just had the youngest, Andrew, still at home…a terrific high-school sophomore involved in sports and band.

Yes indeed, my forties had been happy years, filled with meaning and purpose. But I wasn't sure about turning fifty. The big day in October was only months away. That July things began to go downhill.

The day before I left for my two-week vacation from my job at the radio station, I received a letter from the social security administration. "I don't understand this," I blubbered to the representative on the phone after I tore open the letter.

She responded kindly, "If a minor child only has one living parent, that parent receives financial help from social security only until the child is sixteen. The child continues to receive it until he's eighteen, however."

I hung up the phone in a daze. In four months one-third of my annual income would be gone.

It was too late to cancel the vacation. My daughter in Oakland, California, eagerly awaited our arrival. And besides, I'd painstakingly saved for six months to pay for the trip. Instead of worrying about the future, I repeated my favorite Bible verse over and over: "Commit thy way unto the LORD;

trust also in him; and he shall bring it to pass" (Psalm 37:5).

Thankfully, I didn't know what lay ahead.

The day we arrived in Oakland, a huge portion of one of my back teeth broke into little pieces. Three weeks later, when we returned home and the crown was put in, I had to fork out $487 to my dentist. There was no dental insurance.

The next day I received a bill for the x-rays of my arthritic toe: $144.

The meager medical insurance I could afford didn't cover x-rays—of course.

That same week I noticed I experienced difficulty reading the fine print and sometimes even the medium print. Out of desperation I purchased a huge light for the kitchen that contained four, four-foot-long fluorescent bulbs. It made cooking, bill paying, reading, and letter writing at the kitchen counter much easier for my "approaching-fifty" eyes. But that new light set me back $107.

Next, I made a trip to the optometrist's office. He said both my distance and close-up vision were worsening rapidly.

Naturally, I thought bitterly, as my whole physical well-being flashed before my eyes in bright neon. It screamed, *You're almost fifty, over the hill!*

The bill for the bifocals and reading glasses was $241.

That same week, I finally gave in to one too many

backaches caused by the ancient desk chair in my home office. I figured that my lower back pain was just another pitfall of approaching the big five-o. It was starting to feel like the big five-oh-NO!

Once again, I repeated the verse from the Psalms, stepped out in faith, and wrote a check for $105 for a superb office chair with arms and lumbar support. The day after I put that chair together I noticed a great improvement in my back.

At least my broken tooth was fixed, I could see near and far with my new glasses, my back didn't hurt, and my arthritic toe was feeling better. Things seemed to be looking up.

And then I sat down at my computer to add things up.

Crown for tooth:	$487
X-rays for toe:	$144
Kitchen light:	$107
Bifocals and reading glasses	$241
Desk chair for back pain	$105
TOTAL:	$1,084

I took a deep breath and, once again, committed it all to the Lord.

The next day I discovered that while we were in California, lightning had struck our TV set, rendering it completely useless. I myself could easily do without a TV, but Andrew often brought his friends to our family room to watch movies.

So that week I wrote out another check for a good second-hand TV: $250.

Things were getting out of hand. First, my income was going down by a third, and then suddenly there were all the unexpected bills! I wasn't just going "over the hill" age-wise, I was careening down and out of control, financially as well as physically.

And so I prayed. *Lord...I need a little help down here. Thank You, Lord, for providing for my son and me.* And of course I ended the prayer with my verse from the Psalms.

A few days later while I wallowed in self-pity over my pending birthday, I received a letter from a publisher. As I opened the letter a check tumbled out. The year before I'd written a few short daily devotionals for their annual book, but I'd already been paid for my work the previous spring.

The letter explained that in honor of their twentieth year of publication, they'd turned the distribution of the book over to a larger publisher who expected sales to skyrocket. The original publisher shared the advance on the royalties with all the writers of the book.

My share was $1,338.

All I could do was nod skyward toward Heaven with a banana-sized grin. Then I grabbed my calculator. But even before I added the cost of the TV to my list of five "getting-older" expenses, I knew that the check I held would cover it all.

The bills totaled $1,334, which gave me enough money for all those expenses plus two big juicy cheeseburgers and fries to share with my son.

That night as Andrew and I "chowed down" at his favorite fast-food place, I said what I'd been thinking all day. "Andrew, turning fifty isn't so bad after all. I think my fifties are going to be the best decade yet! I think the Lord will see to it."

THE GOD OF EVERY MAN

YAHOOSKIN FOWLER

You must be born again.

JOHN 3:7 NKJV

I am an American Indian woman from the Northern Paiute Tribe located near Benton, California. Knowing who I am, many people are surprised to learn that I do not have a life history filled with drugs, alcohol, or prison time as many Native Americans do. But as a young girl, I decided that I would not allow these things to control my life.

In the summer of 1960, I was six years old and lived in Fresno, California. At that time, my parents experienced marital problems. Mama wanted Dad to stop drinking and seeing other women. Their arguments grew more heated by the day.

One morning, Mama woke my brother and me up with a big smile. "Get up and get dressed," she said. "We're going to Grandma and Grandpa's house." Soon we were seated on a

"IN HIS LIFE, CHRIST IS AN EXAMPLE, SHOWING US HOW TO LIVE; IN HIS DEATH, HE IS A SACRIFICE, SATISFYING FOR OUR SINS; IN HIS RESURRECTION, A CONQUEROR; IN HIS ASCENSION, A KING; IN HIS INTERCESSION, A HIGH PRIEST."
Martin Luther

Greyhound bus, rolling down the highway. I said to Mama, "Will I ever see Dad again?" Mama assured me that one day I would.

We arrived at the Bishop bus station where Grandma waited. As we traveled the hot, dusty thirty-five miles to her ranch, Grandma kept saying, "Watch for your grandpa. He'll be gathering the cattle." When I finally spotted him, he was riding a big gray horse named Chico—the best cow horse on the vast Pedro Ranch.

With my grandpa, I always felt secure and loved. Grandpa would often sit and have tea parties with me. I could run barefoot and eat all the watermelon I wanted. I attended summer "cow camps" in the mountains and slept under the stars. These were my good memories. However, as time passed, I began to worry about my mom.

She eventually divorced Dad. Over the next eleven years, we went through some very hard times due to Mama's alcoholism and her bad choices in relationships with men. I continued to tell myself to just hang on, hoping things would get better. Grandpa would listen to my worries and tell me to ride my horse over the hills and talk to God. I did that many times, crying out for God to help us.

By the time I was seventeen, Mama had sobered up. She gave me my dad's address and permission to contact him.

However, there was much healing still to come.

Though I had decided to never do the things my parents had done, I married Howdy, a wild rodeo cowboy who willingly embraced the nightlife.

Among the Indian people, we would often hear statements like, "Jesus is a white man's God." I believed this myself. Can you imagine my confusion when Howdy, after a near-death experience, embraced this white man's God? I could not figure out what Howdy was up to this time.

One night while reading his Bible, Howdy told me that God had spoken to him about his future. As he eagerly read the verses to me, I realized that he really believed what he was saying. Pointing my finger in his face, I told him to wake up and quit being stupid. But Howdy said that he had finally found something in life that was real, and he would follow Jesus with or without me.

After Howdy surrendered his life to Jesus, he quit drinking and staying out all night. I was elated, unsure about how long it would last, and yet found myself wanting what Howdy had.

I soon decided to surrender my life to Jesus Christ, and my life changed completely. I experienced an incredible peace. Now, I no longer seek security and happiness, it is now a part of who I am. No longer am I haunted by childhood hurts and disappointments, God has touched my heart.

$\mathcal{T}$HE HEAVEN-SENT CROSS

JULIE PRICE

I will lie down in peace and sleep, for though I am alone,

O Lord, you will keep me safe.

PSALM 4:8 TLB

WE MUST ACT IN SPITE OF FEAR...NOT BECAUSE OF IT.
—*Unknown*

I stood in front of a conference room full of hotel workers in Houston explaining the computerized bookkeeping system my company had created and now sold. I always felt confident teaching training seminars. In fact, my work provided me with stability in a turbulent period in my life: My husband and I were divorcing.

At age thirty-two, I was on my own for the first time. I began to turn to my newly revived faith in God for strength, even as my marriage ended.

I was surprised to see Jim, my boss, slip in the back of the room during my presentation. He motioned to get my attention.

What's wrong? I wondered. I dismissed the class for a short coffee break and then walked over to Jim, who took my elbow and steered me into the lobby.

"Julie, I just got a message from the Sacramento office. The police contacted them to tell you that your house has been broken into and burglarized."

For a moment the news didn't make any sense. Me? A burglary? Why would someone even want to break into my house?

"Don't worry about the rest of the seminar. I'll finish the presentation. You need to get back to Sacramento and talk to the police. Go pack. I'll drive you to the airport when you're ready."

After I thanked him, I headed to my hotel room. I felt a growing sense of personal violation. My house was modest, small—what the broker had called a "starter house." Still, it was my home.

On the drive to the airport, Jim gave me a well-meaning pep talk: "I used to think you were fragile, Julie—that you'd crack under any kind of pressure. But you've proven to be different. You're never intimidated in your presentations, no matter what questions are thrown at you. And even watching you go through this divorce—you've held up like a piece of steel. You're tough. You can handle this. Burglaries happen all the time these days."

Yeah, I thought, *but they don't happen to me all the time!* Sure, I had put up a strong front after Steve left me. But inside I knew I worked to convince myself that I would be okay, that I could take care of myself and live on my own. And now this....

On the flight back to Sacramento I couldn't take my mind off what might have been done to my home, or what the thieves had gone through and taken. It was impossible to place a dollar value on my most-cherished possessions: keepsakes and mementos, sentimental things that could never be replaced. The jewelry box on my dresser contained an out-of-focus snapshot of my mother as a young girl taped inside of the lid. My brother's college ring rested inside of the jewelry box, a ring he had given me for safekeeping while he served time in the Air Force. And the gold cross and chain that my grandmother had presented to my mother when I was a baby. It was small, yet priceless, and knowing it was tucked into the velvet bottom of the jewelry box always made me feel loved and cherished.

In Sacramento I picked up my car at the airport, but while driving home, I became so apprehensive that I pulled over to a pay phone and called my friend Melissa. I asked if she would meet me at my house so that I wouldn't have to face it alone.

When I arrived, I was glad she was there. The sight of my splintered front door behind the crisscrossed yellow crime-scene tape nearly floored me. "Melissa, look at my house...."

"You can get through this, Julie," she said determinedly, tearing the tape away.

My hand shook so badly that I couldn't steady the key, so Melissa reached through the splintered hole in the door and opened it from the inside.

It was even worse than I pictured in my mind. Everything had been overturned, my precious possessions scattered haphazardly on the floor. As we moved slowly down the hall toward my bedroom, I felt as if I were in a dream—although everything was familiar, things still seemed alien somehow. My mattress had been yanked halfway off the bed and now blocked the bedroom doorway. We climbed over it. The intruders had gone through my dresser drawers; my clothes— underwear and all—were strewn around the room. I felt strangely embarrassed. Violated.

Then it struck me. "My jewelry box...." It was gone!

The doorbell rang and I nearly jumped out of my skin. One of the policemen on the case had spotted my car in the driveway. We sat amid the debris in the living room while I made a list of missing property and answered his questions. "You should get that door fixed," the cop advised as he left. "I can't promise we'll catch these guys, and they might come back."

Gee, thanks, I thought, as a cold panicky feeling began to settle in my stomach.

"You'll stay with me tonight," Melissa said as we attempted to straighten up. I didn't have much of a choice. My parents lived in Ohio, and I couldn't just run back to Steve the first time something went wrong. I felt so helpless that I wanted to bang my fists against the wall and scream.

In the morning Melissa made breakfast and I announced plans to go to the hardware store for a new door. "Hang in there!" she called as I drove away.

I picked out the thickest, sturdiest door I could find, and the salesman assured me, "It's our best-seller! It'll really keep out the cold." *I hope it keeps out more than that,* I thought.

"Is your husband going to install it?" the cashier asked brightly as I paid for the new door.

I just nodded. What was the use of explaining? *I'll do it myself,* I thought. *I do everything else for myself these days. How could installing a door be that hard?*

At home I spread a plastic sheet across the patio and laid the door on it. For the next few hours I sanded and varnished, taking great satisfaction in my progress. *This isn't so bad,* I found myself thinking. *I'm doing okay.* While the varnish dried I grabbed lunch, and then studied the instructions on installing the hinges. *Wow, I can do this,* I thought. I felt better already.

I got the hinges on without a problem. Melissa promised to come by for dinner. She could help me mount the door. But there was one more step first—cutting a hole for the doorknob. I dug through the bag of items from the hardware store until I found the tool shown in the directions. *This will be a piece of cake,* I thought.

I made the measurements, lined up the tool with my pencil marks, and began cutting. Almost immediately I heard the horrible, tortured sound of wood splitting. Just like that, with one slip, I had ruined everything.

I hadn't really cried during the last twenty-four hours. I wouldn't let myself, not wanting to look weak and defeated. I made up for it. I sat on the ground in defeat as tears spilled down my face, plopping onto my blue jeans and turning the sawdust into pulp. I had fooled myself into thinking I was strong. *Lord,* I prayed, *I obviously can't take care of myself. Why aren't You helping me?* I thought God was supposed to stay close to me, but I sure didn't feel Him there! I felt abandoned, vulnerable, and alone.

Finally, I wiped my eyes, swept up the mess I'd made, and carried the plastic sheet out to the trash. I angrily stuffed it into the can when, directly at my feet, something gold glinted in the fading sunlight—something familiar and precious: My cross!

I picked up the fragile piece of jewelry and held it in my palm. How had it gotten outside? Of course, there was a practical explanation: It must have fallen out of my jewelry box as the burglars ran off. Yet nothing felt accidental about it. I had never needed my cross the way I needed it at that moment. Tears flooded my eyes again—tears that felt warm and good. "Thank You, Lord," I whispered. "I am sorry for doubting You. You never turn Your back on any of Your children. With You, I am never alone. I can do anything You ask of me."

I put the cross around my neck and walked inside, my step lighter. I called the hardware store to arrange to have someone come and install a new door in the morning. Then I started dinner. Light from the setting sun flooded through my kitchen window. An incredibly reassuring sense of security enveloped me. I was going to be okay. I would stay in my own bed in my own house, safe in the certain knowledge that the Lord was watching over me.

$\mathcal{L}$IVING LIFE GOD'S WAY

After reading these true stories of people who experienced God's grace and power in their lives, perhaps you realize that you are at a point in your own life where you need special help from God.

Are you facing a temptation? A broken relationship? A major disappointment?

Are you ready to experience forgiveness and salvation? Encouragement and hope? Wisdom and inspiration? A miracle?

Though God's power and grace are deep and profound, receiving His help is as simple as ABC.

A—Ask: The only place to start is by asking God for help;

B—Believe: You must believe—have faith—that God can help you;

C—Confess: You must confess—admit—that you truly need God's help to receive it.

Living life God's way doesn't mean that all troubles disappear, but it does mean that there will always be Someone to turn to with all your needs. Call on Him now. For more information on how you can live God's way, visit our website at:

www.godswaybooks.com

$\mathcal{R}$IGHTS AND PERMISSIONS

"A Clear Conscience" © Kitty Chappell. Used by permission.
All rights reserved.

"A Dream Come True" © Christy Sterner. Used by permission.
All rights reserved.

"A Knock on the Door" © Nancy B. Gibbs. Used by permission.
All rights reserved.

"A Marriage Made in Heaven" © Karen R. Kilby. Used by permission.
All rights reserved.

"A Mended Marriage" © Susy Downer. Used by permission.
All rights reserved.

"Anya's Gift" © Renie (Szilak) Burghardt. Used by permission.
All rights reserved.

"A Prayer for Wings" © Shae Cooke. Used by permission.
All rights reserved.

"Be Still with God" © Nancy B. Gibbs. Used by permission.
All rights reserved.

"Connecting with Kyoko" © Lanita Bradley Boyd. Used by permission.
All rights reserved.

"Covered by His Feathers" © Joan Clayton. Used by permission.
All rights reserved.

"Embraced by Prayer" © Christy Sterner. Used by permission.
All rights reserved.

"Falling in Love Again" © Kathryn Lay. Used by permission.
All rights reserved.

"Forgive? Who, Me?" © Candy Arrington. Used by permission.
All rights reserved.

"Given to God" © Linda Henson. Used by permission.
All rights reserved.

"Heaven Sent" © Renie Burghardt. Used by permission.
All rights reserved.

"Her Work Isn't Finished Yet" © Joan Clayton. Used by permission.
All rights reserved.

"I Learned the Truth at Seventeen" © Tonya Ruiz. Used by permission.
All rights reserved.

"I Simply Let Go" © Karen O'Connor. Used by permission.
All rights reserved.

"Lost on Mount Diablo" © Janice Braun Williams. Used by permission.
All rights reserved.

"Miracle in the Rain" © Jan Coleman. Used by permission.
All rights reserved.

"Nifty Fifty" © Patricia Lorenz. Used by permission.
All rights reserved.

"Package Deal" © Gloria Cassidy Stargel. Used by permission.
All rights reserved.

"Pearls of Time" © Karen Majoris-Garrison. Used by permission.
All rights reserved.

"Running in the Rain" © Laura L. Smith. Used by permission.
All rights reserved.

"Smiley" © Karen Majoris-Garrison. Used by permission.
All rights reserved.

"Standing for What I Believed" © Christy Sterner. Used by permission.
All rights reserved.

"The Appearance of Angels" © Elizabeth Bezant. Used by permission.
All rights reserved.

"The Camping Adventure" © Tonya Ruiz. Used by permission.
All rights reserved.

"The Day I Walked into God's Love" © Nancy L. Anderson.
Used by permission. All rights reserved.

"The God of Every Man" © Yahooskin Fowler. From Power to Change.com.
Used by permission. All rights reserved.

"The Heaven-Sent Cross" © Christy Sterner. Used by permission.
All rights reserved.

"The Humbug Holidays and the Lean-To Snowman" © Patricia Lorenz.
Used by permission. All rights reserved.

"The Mirror" © Linda Henson. Used by permission.
All rights reserved.

"The Parable of the Coffee Filter" © Nancy C. Anderson. Used by permission.
All rights reserved.

"The Rose" © Linda Henson. Used by permission.
All rights reserved.

"The Year of the Unexpected" © Melinda Tognini. Used by permission.
All rights reserved.

"Trading the 'Good Life' for the 'Best Life'" © Margolyn Woods.
Used by permission. All rights reserved.

"White Socks" © Jan Wilson. Used by permission.
All rights reserved.

$\mathcal{M}$EET THE CONTRIBUTORS

Nancy C. Anderson has been writing and speaking to women's groups for more than twenty years. She lives near the coastline in Southern California with her husband, Ron, and their teenage son, Nick. She can be contacted at www.nancycanderson.com.

Nancy L. Anderson, the mother of three, is a speaker and writer. She desires to take the message of God's love to all. She can be contacted at: www.e-eaglesrest.com.

Candy Arrington is a freelance author whose publishing credits include *Writer's Digest, Discipleship Journal, Christian Home & School, The Upper Room, Focus on the Family,* and *Spirit-Led Writer.* She is a contributor to *Stories for the Teen's Heart,* Vol. 3 and *Stories from a Soldier's Heart* (Multnomah). She coauthored *Aftershock: Help, Hope, and Healing in the Wake of Suicide* (Broadman & Holman Publishers, 2003). Candy lives in Spartanburg, South Carolina, with her husband, Jim, and their two fantastic teenage children.

Elizabeth Bezant is a West Australian freelance writer, speaker, and writing coach, whose work, both inspirational and educational, has been published around the world. Her business, "writing to inspire.com" empowers, supports, and educates others to reach their true potential. For more information on Elizabeth or her writing please visit www.writingtoinspire.com.

Lanita Bradley Boyd, a former teacher, is now a freelance writer who lives in Fort Thomas, Kentucky. In her writing she draws on her rural childhood, her many years of teaching, her work with churches in a wide variety of ministries, as well as family events and personalities.

Renie Burghardt, who was born in Hungary, is a freelance writer who has contributed to such books as *Chicken Soup for the Horse Lover's Soul, Chicken Soup for the Christian Family Soul, Chocolate for a Woman's Courage, Chocolate for a Teen's Dreams,* and many other anthologies. She lives in the country and enjoys nature, animals, reading, gardening, and spending time with family and friends.

Kitty Chappell is a free-lance writer and speaker. Her full-length book, *Sins of a Father: Forgiving the Unforgivable,* was recently released by New Hope Publishers.

Joan Clayton is the religion columnist for her local newspaper. She has been included three times in *Who's Who Among America's Teachers.* She and her husband, Emmitt, reside in New Mexico.

Jan Coleman has learned to see God in every situation, and it's changed her life. As an author and speaker, she weaves her own personal lessons with biblical insights and inspires readers to embrace life as an adventure with God. Her first book is *After the Locusts; Restoring Ruined Dreams, Reclaiming Wasted Years.* She and her husband, Carl, live in northern California; they love to travel and fish.

Shae Cooke, a Canadian freelance inspirational writer and speaker, contributing author, stay-at-home mother, and former foster child, shares her heart and God's message of hope internationally in print and online. Contact her at shaesy@shaw.ca.

Susy Downer is vice president of DNA Ministries (www.dnaministries.org), based in Chattanooga, Tennessee. Her contributed story is adapted from *Optimize Your Marriage* by Phil & Susy Downer with Ken Walker.

Yahooskin Fowler is an American Indian from the Northern Paiute Tribe located near Benton, California. Her story has been featured online at www.powertochange.com.

Nancy B. Gibbs, the author of four books, is a weekly religion columnist for two newspapers, a writer for *TWINS Magazine,* and a contributor to numerous books and magazines. Her stories and articles have appeared in seven *Chicken Soup for the Soul* books, *Guideposts* books, *Chocolate for Women, Women's World, Family Circle, Decision, Angels on Earth, On Mission Magazine, Happiness,* and many others. Nancy is a pastor's wife, a mother, and a grandmother. She may be reached at daiseydood@aol.com or by writing P.O. Box 53, Cordele, Georgia 31010.

Eva Linda Hays works as a staff nurse in Charlottesville, Virginia. She and her husband, Larry, have nine beautiful, awesome, talented children.

Linda Henson writes for a local newspaper. She has contributed to various anthologies. She is a musician, counselor, and has taught language arts in the public schools.

Karen R. Kilby resides in Kingwood, Texas, with her husband, David. She enjoys sharing her story of God's grace as she speaks for Christian Women's Clubs. She also enjoys helping people understand themselves and others through seminars where she speaks as a Certified Personality Trainer with CLASServices, Inc. founded by Florence and Marita Littauer. She can be contacted at krkilby@kingwoodcable.net.

Kathryn Lay is a full-time writer living in Texas with her family. She has written for *Guideposts, Christian Parenting Today, Discipleship Journal, Decision, Chicken Soup for the Mother's Soul, God Allows U-Turns,* and hundreds of others. She can be reached at rlay15@aol.com or visit her website at http//hometown.aol.com/rlay15/index.html.

Patricia Lorenz is an internationally-known inspirational, art-of-living writer and speaker. She's one of the top contributors to the *Chicken Soup for the Soul* books with twenty stories in fifteen of the titles. She's the author of four books, including her two newest published by Guideposts Books in March, 2004: *Life's Too Short To Fold Your Underwear* and *Grab The Extinguisher, My Birthday Cake's On Fire.* Patricia raised two daughters and two sons and has had kids in college every year for the past 16 years. She lives in Oak Creek, Wisconsin, and says she loves her empty nest and the freedom to follow her dreams while she's still awake!

Karen Majoris-Garrison is an award-winning author, whose stories appear in *Woman's World, Chicken Soup for the Soul* and *God Allows U-Turns.* A wife and mother of two young children, Karen describes her family life as "heaven on earth." You may reach her at innheaven@aol.com.

Karen O'Connor is an award-winning author and speaker from San Diego, California. For more information, visit www.karenoconnor.com.

Tonya Ruiz is a popular speaker and the author of *Beauty Quest, A Model's Journey.* She lives in California with her husband and four teenagers. She may be contacted at www.beautyquest.net.

Laura L. Smith lives in Oxford, Ohio, with her husband and two children. She is the author of the children's book, *Cantaloupe Trees,* as well as many short stories centered on faith.

Christy Sterner is the *God's Way* series editorial consultant and has 10 years of experience in the Christian publishing industry. She has written for many series including *Hugs* and *Chicken Soup for the Soul.*

Melinda Tognini lives in Perth, Western Australia and is an experienced teacher of English and Creative Writing. She has published short fiction, poetry, travel writing and feature articles. She also writes a monthly on-line column for suite101.com. Melinda is currently working on a novel for young adults. She can be reached at togm@ljbc.wa.edu.au.

Janice Braun Williams, horsewoman and writer, lives on a 100-acre ranch in Livermore, California, with her husband, Karl. They have been married thirty-one years and are the parents of six married children. Writing, eleven grandchildren, and a full horse-show schedule, keep Janice busy.

Jan Wilson is the wife of one husband, mother to four children, grandma to one grandson—with another on the way. She's been an RN for 27 years and a Family Nurse Practitioner for nine years. Her writings have been published in the *Journal of Christian Nursing.* She facilitates monthly meetings of the Western Mass Christian Writer's Fellowship in Springfield, Massachusetts. You may contact her at www.scribesnscribblers.com.

Margolyn Woods lives in Oklahoma with her husband, Roy, and their three children. She is a popular speaker at women's retreats and conferences across the country, and the author of eight books. She can be reached at margolyn@cox.net.

ELL US YOUR STORY

Can you recall a person's testimony or a time in your own life when God touched your heart in a profound way? Would your story encourage others to live God's Way? Please share your story today, won't you? God could use it to change a person's life forever.

For Writer's Guidelines, future titles, and submission procedures, visit:

www.godswaybooks.com

Or send a postage-paid, self-addressed envelope to:

God's Way, Editorial
6528 E. 101st Street, Suite 416
Tulsa, Oklahoma 74133-6754

This and other titles in the *God's Way* series
are available from your local bookstore.

God's Way for Fathers
God's Way for Mothers
God's Way for Teens
God's Way for Women

Visit our website at:
www.whitestonebooks.com

*"...To him who overcomes I will give some of the hidden manna to
eat. And I will give him a white stone,
and on the stone a new name written which
no one knows except him who receives it."*

REVELATION 2:17 NKJV

WHITE STONE BOOKS
LAKELAND, FLORIDA